The Organized Academic

The Organized Academic

How to Transform Your Academic Life

Elizabeth A. Wells

ROWMAN & LITTLEFIELD
Lanham • Boulder • New York • London

Published by Rowman & Littlefield
An imprint of The Rowman & Littlefield Publishing Group, Inc.
4501 Forbes Boulevard, Suite 200, Lanham, Maryland 20706
www.rowman.com

86-90 Paul Street, London EC2A 4NE, United Kingdom

Copyright © 2022 by Elizabeth A. Wells

All rights reserved. No part of this book may be reproduced in any form or by any electronic or mechanical means, including information storage and retrieval systems, without written permission from the publisher, except by a reviewer who may quote passages in a review.

British Library Cataloguing in Publication Information Available

Library of Congress Cataloging-in-Publication Data

Names: Wells, Elizabeth Anne, 1964– author.
Title: The organized academic : how to transform your academic life / Elizabeth A. Wells.
Description: Lanham, Maryland : Rowman & Littlefield, 2022. | Includes bibliographical references and index. | Summary: "This book offers realistic day-to-day techniques that promise to transform your academic life"— Provided by publisher.
Identifiers: LCCN 2022023350 (print) | LCCN 2022023351 (ebook) | ISBN 9781475867985 (cloth) | ISBN 9781475867992 (paperback) | ISBN 9781475868005 (epub)
Subjects: LCSH: College teaching—Vocational guidance. | College teachers—Professional relationships.
Classification: LCC LB1778 .W39 2022 (print) | LCC LB1778 (ebook) | DDC 378.1/25—dc23/eng/20220713
LC record available at https://lccn.loc.gov/2022023350
LC ebook record available at https://lccn.loc.gov/2022023351

In Memoriam Linda M. Wells
A great teacher

Contents

Acknowledgments ix

Introduction xi

1 Know Thyself 1

2 Time 13

3 Writing 33

4 Teaching 49

5 Nuts and Bolts 67

6 Life 85

Postscript 95

Bibliography 99

Index 101

About the Author 105

Acknowledgments

A book like this one is many years in the making, and it is the product of countless hours inside and outside the classroom, experimenting with different techniques and strategies to make the academic life work. First and foremost, then, I am indebted to my students, colleagues, and the countless people I have coached and led in workshops, who have given me not only the fodder for this book but the many questions, complaints, and issues that I have had to address with those many good people. I am particularly grateful that I was granted an administrative leave after my stint as dean of arts at Mount Allison University which allowed me the time and focus to write this book and to get it into publication in a short amount of time. Further, I am lucky to have had great people read and comment on the manuscript: Rob Haskins, Jeremy Grimshaw, Jessica Riddell, and Eileen Herteis. This book would not have been possible without my editors, Sarah Kaye Klapman (who could almost be called a coauthor of this book with the tremendous care she has taken in editing my often rambling prose), and Developmental Editor Carol Wells, who treated the manuscript with exquisite care and pointed out all the places of inconsistency, lack of clarity, and aspects of tone. Gibson J. MacMillan has edited and provided logistical and technical assistance to carry out the tasks I could not do myself. My indexer, Ruth Pincoe, a veteran of my work, did an excellent job of indexing such a short book on a very narrow topic.

My mentors are many, but I have not met any of them: David Allen, Chris Bailey, Cal Newport, Stephen Covey, Julie Morgenstern, and many others have informed my practice around administrative organization and have provided many hours of thought-provoking material which has shaped my approach to this field.

Introduction

HOW I BECAME THE ORGANIZED ACADEMIC

When I was in graduate school, many years ago, my group of friends came up with the (hilarious) imagined schedule of an ideal grad student, which we called "The Day of the Perfect Person." This ideal academic awoke naturally at 6:00 a.m., feeling refreshed and looking so good that she did not need a drop of makeup. She toted her organic homemade lunch to school, finished all her assignments with ease, and relaxed in the evening by snuggling her dog and taking long walks with her perfect, adoring boyfriend. She never wasted time, didn't check email very much, and breezed through life carefree and productive. It was a funny blow-by-blow account of what it would be like to have it all.

Our reality was quite different: snoozing the alarm clock, foraging for a piece of last night's pizza, and endlessly checking email and pulling all-nighters while worrying about what our advisers wanted or what grades we would get. Although those were heady days in many ways, some people in academia are still living our grad school life, burned out, behind the eight ball, and worried now about tenure and promotion and the difficult student in that 9:30 class. All the while, we imagine everyone else must be living the life of the perfect person, day after day. *Surely*, we think, *no one else has the life I have*. Regardless of where you are on the organization spectrum, you may have picked up a book called *The Organized Academic* hoping that it will turn you into that perfect student, now turned professor. It will solve all your problems and make this year different from every other year. Unfortunately, that is not what this book is about, nor what it can promise. However, it does compile one compatriot's years of knowledge (and mistakes) inside and outside of the classroom and pass the summary on like a good mentor does to an advisee. Many of us have been there, and we've learned—sometimes the hard way—how to make academic life work. For the past several years, I have been a full-time academic in a small liberal arts university while personally coaching professors and graduate students, both in groups and individually, on how to improve their teaching and research practices. I've learned a lot from these experiences and from these wonderful people, and now I'd like to share that knowledge with more members of my profession. *The Organized Academic* is not about perfection but about doing the best you can with what you have right now and looking at making your career a more enjoyable, less stressful experience. This is important work that I feel called to do.

When I talk to most academics, no matter what stage of their career, they express three overriding emotions that they find difficult to overcome: guilt, shame, and fear. They feel guilty that they are not getting everything done to their satisfaction, to the best of their abilities, or to the expectations of others. They feel ashamed that they are not able to meet all their commitments to themselves and others. And they feel afraid that people will find out they are imposters, that they don't "know it all." To compound this, we often feel guilt, shame, and fear about our guilt, shame, and fear. We feel guilty that we can't meet our own or others' expectations, we feel ashamed that we have this great career with lots of time and freedom but are still stressed and overworked, and we fear that others will find out how far behind we are—especially when compared with other, seemingly more successful, professors. I can say that I have not encountered a single academic who does not experience at least one of these emotions on a regular basis, and I find it particularly pronounced among the most successful in our field. Does that mean we are all incompetent and disorganized poseurs? Not at all. We have simply chosen a profession in which our work is never done. We can never know enough, write enough, teach well enough, or publish enough. I have found that even highly decorated senior academics who have reached full professorship and have nothing left to prove put in late nights in their studies, driven to produce more and more, be more accessible and helpful—in effect, to be the perfect academic. The problem is we never get there.

Introduction

Although this book will hopefully give you some ideas as to how to become more efficient and effective with less stress and fatigue, I cannot remove these feelings from your life because they were installed by a graduate school system that is not built for modern life. We are no longer predominantly male professors with wives at home who type up our manuscripts and get dinner on the table. Nor do we usually have a raft of graduate or teaching assistants who can do our grading while we stare out the window or sit at our desk having the Big Thoughts. We live complicated lives, and the expectations that have been placed on faculty in this modern age are higher than they have ever been before, all with less support than we have ever had before. This occupation is not for the fainthearted. However, with some trimming here and some efficiencies there, we can have a more enjoyable life in the academy without giving up everything of ourselves to our institutions.

To start with, we need to get rid of our guilt, shame, and fear. The longer I work with people, either in group workshops or one-on-one, the more compassion I have for the modern academic and the more confidently I can assure you that your feelings are natural and universal. Once you accept that you will not know it all, write it all, and teach it all, you will be a much happier and more relaxed professional. I know this is not an easy thing to let go; some counseling or support groups in universities would be great ways for us to decompress, tell stories, and share practices. But we are all too afraid to show weakness. Weakness is rewarded neither in graduate study nor in pre-tenure faculty. However, I hope that this book will provide you with a quiet place to retreat and think deeply about how you do what you do—and how you could do it a little bit better.

For those of us living it, academic life can feel like an unusual combination of freedom and constriction. As professors, we have significant flexibility as to when and where we do our work. At the same time, we often have crushing and unrealistic deadlines, our students expect us to be constantly available, either in person or electronically, and our work is never "done." There is always more we should know, more we should research, and more we should write. Of all occupations, we are the least likely to "retire" when we retire, because we often care so passionately about the things we research that we don't ever want to stop thinking and writing about them. But despite the general public's impression that we work eight hours a week and have the summers off, we in the profession know that we work far more than many who have equivalent education and often for less money and less recognition. You have to really love this job to do it, and I hope this book helps you find a way to love it more, and do it better, than you ever have before, all with improved work/life balance.

As someone who likely has an advanced degree yourself, you may wonder why you should listen to me, a fellow academic, about how to run your professional life. To answer that, let me tell you what I have accomplished over fifteen years: I was hired before I finished my doctorate, something that is unheard of now but was still possible when I entered the job market. I was granted early tenure, and I achieved full professorship early. My research has won two national disciplinary awards, one for my dissertation, which was judged one of the most promising in North America (this is when I was still in graduate school), and one on the book version, which was awarded the best book in its field some years later. I have won five teaching awards, including two in my university, one in my region, and a national teaching award, the 3M National Teaching Fellowship, which is awarded to ten best professors across my country in all disciplines. I then won the teaching award from my professional discipline. My various projects have been fully funded, including my dissertation. I am called upon by people in my discipline for committee work and am invited to give papers on a regular basis, and I get work published in good journals regularly. I have presented or published over seventy papers in these years. I am well-liked by students, and many have said that my teaching and mentorship have had a deep impact on them. As a result, I won my university's top award for productivity and a well-balanced career, culminating in a public lecture during which I vowed to change my entire discipline through my scholarship. I still enjoy my colleagues, students, and the town in which I live. This would seem like success by usual academic standards.

However, I felt called to administration. After tenure, I became head of my department, which is a music department in a small, liberal arts college. Headship or chairship of such a department is not what one usually thinks about in a typical university; it involves knowing about and maintaining various musical instruments, running a concert hall, organizing a series of over eighty concerts and events every academic year, recruiting and admitting students, advising those students, running the marketing and communications angles of the department, and doing quotidian things like managing faculty, courses, resources, and relationships with the rest of the university community. I did this job for five years, and as a result sat on fifty committees and working groups, ran numerous searches, and dealt with all the problems and issues that come up in the close-knit liberal arts community. Beyond administering my department, I also sat on a large number of committees across the institution, acting as faculty council secretary, and then took on a five-year role elected as the secretary of senate. Later, I was named dean of arts, a role that I served in for two-and-half years. My service to the university was deemed "outstanding" by my former dean, and I had—fortunately—no enemies. For those who have never been in upper administration, the degree of dysfunction and distress that comes across one's desk every day would be hard to imagine. It is a 24/7 job. During my time as both dean and faculty member, I sent 107,000 emails.

Beyond the university, I have also given thirty-six service talks about all aspects of my research, teaching, and other work background (I was a radio producer and a stage manager, partly during grad school, before I took up my first academic position). I chaired the Council of 3M National Teaching Fellows, cofounded an International Federation of National Teaching Fellows, and also earned a certificate in college and university administration along the way to further my administrative skill set. I did more, and more often, than most people I knew.

But I also had a life outside of the university: I volunteered or sat on the boards of the local music festival, a professional theater company, and an early music festival and volunteered for three programs for the Red Cross. I trained as a Hospice palliative care volunteer, was the president of the local charitable association, and was certified as a first-aider and a first responder. I studied for, and was ordained as, a deacon in my faith community, which also takes some of my time, including Sunday services. This all did not go unnoticed. I have been interviewed on national radio seven times and have been featured in *University Affairs*, *Maclean's*, the *Globe & Mail* University Report, *Times/Transcript*, *Telegraph Journal*, *Rochester Review*, and *Trinity Alumni Magazine*. *Huffington Post* called my Beatles course one of the "Coolest Courses in Canada."

What about my personal life? I've watched every episode of every television show I'm interested in (full runs of 11 entire series so far), I work out 1.5 hours 5 or 6 days a week, and I sleep 9 hours a night. I also prepare most of my meals, which are very healthy, and I file my taxes by February 15 every year. I socialize with people and have fun, entertain often, and enjoy wine in the evenings in front of the fire. By all accounts, I have built a great personal life. Although I have health challenges, as many people do, I manage them well with medication and exercise. To the point I made earlier, then, this is as successful as I think a young- to middle-career academic can be, and perhaps this level of personal and professional success is something you already enjoy. However, I have the blood pressure and cholesterol of a teenager, according to my physician, and I am happy and contented with my life. I consider myself a relaxed and "low-energy" person.

I have all my courses prepped a year in advance, with complete PowerPoints, lecture notes, and uploaded course material. I get my reserve lists and book orders to the bookstore completed on this same time line. My office is tidy (although I allow that a certain amount of occasional chaos is good for academic life), and I am on time or early for every appointment and every committee I sit on. In my administrative work, I have usually been ahead of deadline and am waiting for someone else to do something before I can take a next step on projects. I never pull an all-nighter or have to work wildly on an intense schedule to get things done. Basically, I have a sane schedule, and I am working often months in advance of where most people are. I even decide ahead of term what I'm going to wear every day. Although that last one is a bit much for most people, imagine what it would be like if you never had to think about what you put on in the morning. Am I a perfect academic? No. But I'm organized, and that's what makes all the difference.

So, how did I achieve all this in this time frame, with a calm mind and a healthy body? That's what this book was designed to show you—and how you can do it, too. I've been giving workshops on workflow, time management, and productivity for small groups of people, but I'd like to share what I've learned with the wider academic community and let you know that there is hope. You don't have to be overwhelmed, overworked, and overtired. This book will help you to:

1. take steps to refine what you are doing, define it to yourself and others, and make sure that your work aligns with your values and objectives;
2. identify pressing problems around time, energy, and work/life balance in getting work done;
3. provide exercises for considering research, teaching, service missions, focus, and goals;

4. suggest best practices in time management and workflow applicable to academic life;
5. offer some basic sources and further reading;
6. create opportunities for independent work so that you can use whatever practices, ideas, or techniques are most valuable to you after you finish the book; and
7. create Mihaly Csikszentmihalyi's sense of "flow"—that whatever you are doing at any given time is exactly what you should be doing.

I'll provide some caveats up front so you know what to expect and what not to expect from this book. This is not career advice. Everyone's path is so different, with so many unavoidable diversions, that I can't predict whether what I am offering will be appealing or relevant. I also don't want to contradict any advice from your union or faculty association. These groups not only look out for your best interests but also—through collective agreements—define your workloads and responsibilities. I am not a "career coach," although I have been coached by some high-flying consultants. I am a working academic, in the trenches with you. My advice comes from lived experiences, not theories or systems (although I will be writing about many such systems in the coming pages). Despite drawing from a number of different writers and thinkers in this book, this is not a scholarly or scientific study. It is peer mentorship. I will be taking many of my examples from my own teaching and research life, because I can speak best about my own experiences. Whether you are in a large research institution, a small liberal arts college like mine, or somewhere in the middle, many of the techniques and ideas will hopefully be helpful to you.

When there are so many self-help and time management books on the market, why do we need one for academics? Can't we just get a good day planner and take it from there? In a word, no. The university world and culture are unique to North America. We are somewhere between a government organization, a business, and a belief organization (remember, universities in the Western world grew out of the Catholic Church). We have jobs—and values—that are not reflected in corporate culture, and we usually respond negatively to the idea that the university should be run as a kind of business. Without getting into that debate, the truth is that our lives and jobs are mostly incomprehensible to others (even people in our own institutions), so we need a way of understanding our work and our values. Although we are often considered the most educated people in our society, we are never taught how to run our work lives as academics. Sure, graduate school teaches us how to write and do research. Sometimes we are taught something about teaching. But we are never taught how to do service, how to sit on a committee, or how to "do" the academic job, which is not at all like grad school. As much as we may reject the language and mores of the business world, there are things we can learn from their methodologies. We still have "deliverables"—the lecture needs to happen at 10:30 a.m. on Monday, and the manuscript has its deadline. We can learn from our colleagues in the "real world" about productivity, efficiency, and elegance. We just need to translate what we learn into our own terms.

My Methodology

Although you will find many of my own ideas in this book, you will notice that my systems are undergirded by four important books that have literally changed my life and the way I work. The first one I read was Stephen Covey's *The Seven Habits of Highly Effective People*. This was published in 1989 and went viral in the business world, as well as among high flyers in a number of other disciplines. Although I got a lot from the habits themselves, Covey's 1995 *First Things First* was the book that put his ideas into a practical framework for time management and mission development. You will find that the portions of this book based on mission are heavily influenced by Covey's ideas and systems. Julie Morgenstern's *Organizing from the Inside Out* and *Time Management from the Inside Out* contain exceptional ideas on blocks of time or space. Morgenstern was a harried mother of a young child who was completely disorganized. Trying to take her young daughter out for a walk one day, she found that just getting all the gear she needed together left no time for the walk itself. Galvanized by this experience, she got herself organized and went on to write three books and start a large consulting company where she trains people to organize others. My ideas around the best times of day to do certain tasks are taken directly from Morgenstern's work.

However, the biggest influence on my thinking and my own productivity has been the work of David Allen, whose book *Getting Things Done* has changed the lives of many people, including academics. A personal organizational and productivity consultant, Allen wrote the book in the late 1990s to bring his particular brand of organizational ethos to a wider audience. It has since spawned an entire movement called simply "GTD." Especially popular in the tech industries, Allen's work has also found purchase among academics, with its emphasis on focusing on what's in your head and right in front of you, instead of using your brain to try to manage the number of overwhelming tasks that we all have to deal with. More than any other writer, Allen's work has affected me deeply, and you will find his fingerprints throughout this book.

In the last year, I discovered Cal Newport's series of books, everything from his youthful forays into getting ahead in college (*How to Win at College* and *How to Become a Grade A Student*) to his later *So Good They Can't Ignore You*. However, his *Deep Work* of 2016 literally changed my life. It is so important for professors to read this book that I gift it to everyone I know. An academic himself (he teaches computer science), this remarkable young scholar has earned tenure and continues productively teaching and researching while writing four books "on the side" for a general audience. Amazingly, he also turns off the computer at 5:30 p.m. and goes home to his wife and kids to have a life. There is much to admire about Newport but even more to glean from his well-researched and easy-to-read guides on productivity and focus. In our world of digital hyper-communication and information overload, Newport has a lot to teach. His recent *Digital Minimalism* is another powerful tool for taming the electronic dragon. Newport also runs a blog directed at college students, but with insights we can all use in our academic lives. There are many more thinkers who have influenced my ideas over the years, but what you hold in your hands right now is the adaptation of all these methods into my own special brand of time management and productivity. I urge you to read these books if you can, but what I have tried to do is give you the kernels of their wisdom along with my own ideas and strategies around academic life.

Knowledge Work

Why are our jobs so hard to define? It's because most of us in the academy fall under the category of "knowledge work." This means that, for the most part, we deal with ideas and the expression and dissemination of those ideas. Although many might do field or lab work, we generally do more thinking, talking, writing, and teaching than we do manual labor. This is still hard going. It takes time, energy, focus, and even a certain amount of physical fortitude. The products of our work are usually emails, reports, class lectures, and, of course, publications. But because most of us don't make something concrete, it's harder to corral all the information, inputs, and tasks before us. So, as David Allen would say, we have to spend some time "defining our work." Defining work is not exactly like planning, but it does involve an element of planning that is vitally important. Most of us only consider ourselves "working" when we are actually writing, grading, or lecturing. The rest of our time can spill dangerously close to "having fun"—reading a fascinating book or article, learning a new software program, and so on. But any time you are thinking about work, you are working. Most academics, when defined this way, are working most of the day whether they feel like it or not. But this thinking, this ruminating, and turning ideas over and over is part of what we must do to produce our best work. Part of doing the work well requires actually defining what our work *is*. This means that I don't want you to consider that the yearly, weekly, and even daily basis I suggest is somehow "wasting time" or only "preparing to work." Planning is what allows us to be effective in doing the work that "counts," like the writing and teaching that makes up the majority of our workday. The two secrets to managing in academia, then, are advanced planning and defining your own work. In this book, I will go through a series of stages to define and then do the work that flow logically from one to another.

In chapter 1, I will ask you to answer the most important question you can, which is why you are doing this demanding job in the first place. We need to understand our roles, motivations, and values before we begin defining our work. If we don't have this part figured out, we may spend days, months, and even years of our lives doing work that is not ultimately meaningful or important to us or others. This chapter will also ask you to get in touch with your patterns around energy and time. Knowing yourself, then, is your first task. In chapter 2, we will delve into academic time and how to best organize the days, weeks, and months of the academic year. This is where you will find the most traditional "time management" advice, and this section can probably be used by anyone who is looking for a better way to allot their energy and resources.

In chapter 3, I will cover the essentials of finding time, energy, and focus for writing or what we think of as the "academic" knowledge work that lies outside of teaching and service. Most academics claim they need more of this type of time, and so here I try to give you some ideas and resources for maximizing it. Chapter 4 deals with the all-important role of teaching in our daily lives and how classroom and course management can make this a much less stressful experience. Here I bring to bear what I have learned about syllabus design, lecture preparation, and grading.

Chapter 5 is called "Nuts and Bolts" and contains much of my general knowledge about academic life, from travel to working in archives, from using checklists and rubrics to various other tools of the trade. Chapter 6 revolves around "life," that elusive thing that we do on the odd occasion when we are not working. This is an important part of being human that many academics neglect or let fall into chaos. In this chapter, I share some ideas that I have found helpful to organize and de-stress my life outside of the academy.

Although you can read the chapters in any order, I recommend working through the book in order or at least starting with the "Know Thyself" chapter before delving into any other sections. An old academic joke goes that if you are stuck writing your thesis, then "read another book." In this case, I hope that the following chapters give you the impetus you need to write the thesis, the book, the article, or just to make your academic life a little bit easier.

Chapter 1

Know Thyself

There are many days when harried academics might ask themselves, "Why am I here? Why am I doing this difficult job in the first place?" The journey toward an organized and effective work life starts by understanding what drives people to do what they do. What are our values, our ideals? What are we trying to achieve? The best way to get at this is to go through a thoughtful process of discernment on mission. The term "mission statement" makes some people cringe given the corporate flavor it has absorbed (think pleasing customer-directed statements in hotel lobbies, etc.). However, like many things borrowed from the corporate world, thinking about why we are doing what we are doing and what our ultimate goals may be is helpful in aligning work with deeper values. Certainly, too, if we did not learn very much beyond how to do research in our graduate programs, no one taught us to do a deep dive into what we are doing in this occupation in the first place.

Academics are accustomed to writing teaching philosophy statements and programs of research. These are often fairly straightforward documents. A philosophy statement will describe methods, practices, and underlying assumptions of one's teaching, with examples. A program of research will lay out plans for the next several years, with certain publishing goals in mind, and also communicate general methodologies, philosophical underpinnings, and the trajectory of ongoing research activities. Each one is generally two to three pages long, and these documents are used for specific purposes: tenure and promotion, grant applications, or nominations for awards. A philosophy or research statement may provide a basis for actions and a description of them. A mission statement instead underlies each of these documents and provides the guiding principles that dictate those actions. A mission is not based on the everyday activities but concerns ultimate objectives. Therefore, it is not long and detailed but instead provides helpful, guiding statements.

Why, when there are so many other pressing concerns, start with a mission? The most important reason is that it defines core values and determines drives. Why have we chosen this particular topic or discipline, and why is it exciting? What is our raison d'être, our profile? How will we assert what we need for our own academic life and safeguard it against so many other pressures? Most importantly, a mission helps align goals and values with the work we take on. This redirects time and energy to the most essential things, and then goals can flow from those instead of coming from other places or people. A mission helps us to make hard decisions, and on challenging days we can take it out, read it, and be inspired. However, one mission statement is not enough to define everything we are—we really need several. True, for some people, one overarching life mission can be very powerful. This often entails spiritual or philosophical ideas that govern how one goes about life on this planet. But for most people, it is best to have mission statements for each part of working life: teaching, research, service, and maybe even "career."

An overarching plan can be quite helpful—and is suggested—but to make decisions on the ground and in the moment, separate missions need to be explored. They can be developed individually; however, they need to align. Having a mission to homeschool small children and be the most present parent possible may not align with being constantly in demand as a keynote presenter all over the world, for example. Make sure that the missions support and do not contradict each other.

Stephen Covey was the master of the mission; he felt that unless we "begin with the end in mind" and know exactly why we are doing what we are doing, we are swimming in uncharted waters and letting other people and factors control what we do. We are not practicing "first things first." However, others argue that we have enough on our plates already and that adding another patina of "values" is going to give us even more to do and complicate our lives unnecessarily. As a middle ground, a well-crafted and considered mission can help in making day-to-day decisions and prove useful in deciding where to direct attention.

Covey teaches that there are several key components in a mission statement. It should address core values, things we want to learn, and the legacy that we want to leave. It should identify core strengths and areas of our life or career that need work, describe how we are at our very best, and detail negative things about ourselves that we need to monitor. In Covey's *First Things First*, he takes the reader through a series of exercises to identify these components. On the Franklin-Covey website (the Franklin Planner company joined with the Covey methodology), their "mission builder" software has a space to plug in these various components and then generate a mission. Instructions are provided there on how to create missions for teams, families, businesses, and individuals. However, some values are specific to academic life and are worth focusing on.

Core values for research and teaching might fall under these rubrics:

Rigor: Although we'd all like to think our academic work has some element of rigor, for some people this is the most important aspect of their work.

Autonomy or Independence: There are academics who find that the originality and autonomy of their thinking is the most important part of their work. They don't want to be seen as following or building on the work of others but instead as striking out in bold new directions.

Interdependence: These individuals value the work they do as coexisting in a larger scholarly debate in which they are just one voice. The connection the work has with that of others may be its most important asset.

Service: Some people feel that their work is a form of service to the wider community, whether that is other researchers, their university community, or society at large.

Level of Influence: Others would like to be the most highly regarded expert in their area, whether that be an entire discipline or a subgroup. Level of achievement, respect, and notoriety are important to these scholars.

Feminism/Environmental: For example, some people may do what they do through a feminist or environmental lens, and their work is designed to benefit specific groups of people or the planet.

These are just a few of the core values that characterize a relationship to work and what makes it important. What are our values as teachers? Compassion, passion, rigor, standards, communication, feminism, and political action can be guiding values in a teaching practice. They should be considered when crafting a teaching mission. After determining four or five key values, consider strengths and weaknesses. What are strengths in teaching, research, service, career, or any other parameter that seems appropriate? What components in each of these areas need work or to be carefully monitored? Answering these questions will form the backbone of various missions. Covey includes a series of questions (on pp. 107–109 of *First Things First*) that could be asked at a person's eightieth birthday. Probably a more relevant version for academics is to imagine what we would like people to say about us at our retirement party. In their speeches and farewell commentary, what would we like our students to say about us? Our faculty or departmental colleagues? Our disciplinary colleagues? And, finally, what would we like to see as our most significant accomplishment? These are not rhetorical questions.

Here is a teaching mission statement, taken from a teaching philosophy:

> Teaching is a human endeavor. As much as we value the mastery of information and skills, and their application, what we as teachers and students truly desire is to be educated, the result of embracing values and attitudes that transcend the material we study. What I try to shape through teaching is not results but the values of *people* with whom we want to live, work, and share our world. This endeavor—to create thoughtful, critical, compassionate and passionate individuals—crosses all disciplines, all methodologies, all approaches, and is the foundation of my teaching. (Emphasis in original).

This idea, one of compassionate humanism, underlies everything the writer does as a teacher. It directs how she designs courses, what courses she chooses to teach, how she conducts her classrooms and develops class assignments, and how she deals with students. She never wavers from this series of values, which helps her make decisions as to how and where to dedicate time and energy. This is her research mission statement:

> To explore the intersections of human life and music and music-making in a way that enriches the world's knowledge and appreciation of musical works and their context. Through mindful and important pieces of scholarship to reveal unknown or underappreciated musics or to shed new and thought-provoking light on others. It is my mission to continually improve my critical, analytical and writing skills to create scholarship on the highest level of relevance and interest.

This is a research mission for someone who works on some popular but also some marginalized musical repertoire, and so the mission is twofold: to uncover marginalized work and to shed light on well-known work.

That may all seem well and good, but how does this play out in everyday life? How would we actually use one of these mission statements?

In the first instance, having a mission like this helps in making decisions about what projects to take on and how much time to devote to teaching and research. It helps prioritize between different projects and goals. Most importantly, these missions would undergird a research statement or a teaching philosophy statement. They provide the bones or the structure; personal details flesh them out. The author of the above mission submitted a manuscript on a long-neglected repertoire of music to a major publisher. The editor liked the work but after sending it out to readers remarked that the press would like to know how this would relate to a wider audience. The question became whether it would be right for this particular work to be "popularized" in this way or if the goal to "reveal unknown or "underappreciated musics" was being sabotaged. After some consideration, it became clear that this particular repertoire, if approached in a different way, actually informed thinking on much more famous pieces of music. When slanting the research and writing in this way, it was possible to do both things, thus fulfilling the second part of the value statement, "to shed new and thought-provoking light on others." Although the author eventually went to another press with the book, this thinking process allowed her to ask if she was really fulfilling her research mission with the manuscript as it presently stood. And, in the end, it became a better book.

When writing a research or teaching statement, it is easiest to start with the short mission and then let the statement flow from it. The teaching mission included above flows from the earlier teaching philosophy statement. This is a good way to see if the alignment of our values and interests truly feeds into what we are doing in our research or how we teach. What do we do, however, if we find that what we are doing is not in line with these values and goals? Most professors have taken on far too much both in terms of work and commitments. We must take a good, hard look at every research project, every course, and every service commitment that we have accepted. Then we can be ruthless in eliminating everything that does not accord with our mission. This is a sobering, but also liberating, process.

What about a service mission? For most people, university service is just something that people "do"—most often find themselves on committees or working groups that have been foisted upon them by others. As much as this is often the case, we can align our interests in service as well. Passionate about the welfare of students? Why not sit on a committee that looks at student mental health? Feel that standards are not high enough in the research community? Work toward getting a spot on a funding body or research ethics board that polices such standards. If organizing things is a personal strength, and events are a highlight of the school year, consider organizing a conference. Interests and talents together are a powerful combination. Do not wait to be asked; instead, proactively think about service interests and go after those committees. Colleagues will be surprised but also delighted to see one of their own step forward for opportunities that usually require strong-arming people into taking them up. It is helpful to create a service mission along with missions for teaching and research that provide space to explore our own innate interests. The resulting work will be more joyful and productive as a result.

Here is Gandhi's mission:

"Let the first act of every morning be to make the following resolve for the day:

- I shall not fear anyone on Earth.
- I shall fear only God.
- I shall not bear ill will toward anyone.
- I shall not submit to injustice from anyone.
- I shall conquer untruth by truth.
- And in resisting untruth, I shall put up with all suffering."

Not all of us can match that in terms of grandeur and simplicity, but we can make our lives more focused (and ultimately, more organized) by asking ourselves these very important questions about why we do what we do. Talking to other people who know us and our work very well will give us a better sense of our values and goals. Then consider a retreat or just a few hours in a coffee shop to work out the details of the mission and condense it into the simplest and most straightforward language possible. Although seasoned academics will find this a much easier process, everyone can do this work profitably. Don't be surprised, however, if this process sparks a series of career-related changes.

GOALS

There are few things that are more important in the academic life than to know our goals, our limits, and how we do our best work. Many people stumble through the week rushing from one urgent commitment or task to another, without prioritizing or thinking about whether what they are doing is the best thing for that particular moment. Knowing personal rhythms and cycles of energy makes this process much easier to manage and allows for more efficient and stress-free days. At its simplest, time management in the academy is energy and focus management. We all have the same number of hours in the day, but we need to reserve the times when we have the most focus and energy for the most demanding activities. The second part of "knowing thyself" then is to figure out how we work as individuals; this will allow us to tailor our now well-honed missions into action.

In her books *Organizing from the Inside Out* and *Time Management from the Inside Out*, Julie Morgenstern likens the areas of a home to the areas of a kindergarten classroom: there is the dress-up area, the painting area, the reading area, and so on. In the same way, when writing about time, she designates times of day as reflective of different energy cycles and personal proclivities for getting certain tasks done. Adapting her exercise for the academic life, consider the following:

Morning is the best time for me to:
And the worst time for me to:
Afternoon is the best time for me to:
And the worst time for me to:
Evening is the best time for me to:
And the worst time for me to:

There are general kinds of activities or areas that can be imagined here:

- Sleep
- Socialize
- Family time/kids
- Read, listen to music, watch TV for pleasure
- Cook
- Housework/laundry/yardwork
- Exercise

- Relationship
- Errands/shopping
- Meditate/journal
- Bathe

For example, some people find that they can't start the day without a hot shower to wake them up and get them going. Other people find a hot bath at the end of the workday is a tonic that helps them get more done at night or relaxes them before bed. Exercise has additional benefits at different times of day. Morning is when testosterone is higher and there is less likelihood of injury. Some prefer to work out after work when they have a little more flexibility with their time. The same can be said for almost anything on this list. Think through some of these basic life activities first and then turn to the recurring tasks that take place in academic life. Although it seems that our work can include a multitude of activities, when broken down into an itemized list, there is a finite number of task types that people do as academics. For instance:

Humanities Activities:

- Writing new prose
- Editing prose
- Bibliographic searching and management
- Reading primary or source documents for general background
- Reading primary or source documents to analyze or take extensive notes
- Reading secondary source documents for general context
- Reading secondary source documents to analyze or take extensive notes
- Reading in closest areas to my project
- Reading in general area of my project
- Managing, creating, or sorting pictures, illustrations, diagrams, or examples
- Writing or editing abstracts
- Writing or editing proposals for conferences
- Managing paperwork re conferences
- Reading disciplinary e-lists or discussion boards
- Updating CV and preparing funding reports or year-end evaluation data
- Searching for funding opportunities

- Writing grant applications (can be huge depending on discipline)
- Proofreading galleys, and so on
- Social science: designing, implementing, and analyzing data
- Thinking (also known as "staring out the window")

Science Activities:

- Designing experiments
- Training students on experimental techniques
- Conducting and/or supervising experiments
- Analyzing and synthesizing data
- Writing manuscripts
- Mentoring students and postdocs
- Reviewing scientific manuscripts
- Mentoring students in writing/editing scientific manuscripts
- Reviewing grants (NSERC, CIHR, CFI, etc.)
- Writing grants
- Planning fieldwork and its logistics
- Preparing conference presentations and poster sessions (including student training)
- Spending money (putting out tenders, meeting with vendors, testing and assessing equipment and consumables, etc.)

Teaching Activities (All Disciplines):

- Designing class outlines or plans
- Designing and testing laboratory exercises
- Creating the detailed content of class plans and lectures
- Reviewing notes/class activities to prep class
- Lecturing/running class
- Emailing related to courses with students, head, registrar, and so on
- Completing paperwork related to courses with all of the above (submitting syllabi and forms)
- Grading
- Submitting or recording grades and creating or maintaining class lists and grade sheets

Meeting with students, ad hoc or planned

- Spending time online re course management system, posting assignments, and so on

- Attending meetings in department or with colleagues related to teaching or curriculum
- Solving problems (unruly students, plagiarism cases, logistical mix-ups, technology failure, etc.)
- Thinking (also known as "stare out the window")

Service Activities:

- Reviewing articles or book prospects as a referee or outside assessor
- Reviewing tenure or promotion files as an outside assessor
- Editing a scholarly journal
- Participating in activities related to sitting on boards or committees within discipline
- Attending senate or all-faculty meetings
- Attending departmental meetings
- Attending ad hoc meetings on other subjects
- Reading administrative emails and memos (policies, procedures, events, and announcements)
- Various work items stemming from meetings (writing a report, drafting a recommendation, and planning a party)
- Writing student reference letters
- Writing faculty or colleague reference letters
- Organizing conferences and similar events
- Solving problems (can't access meeting notes, double-booked meetings, computer crashes, etc.)
- Thinking (i.e., staring out the window)—particularly if you have a heavy service load or are an administrator

This may seem like a reductive list, but virtually everything people do as academics can be lumped under one of these categories. Realistically, there are only three major activities to do around teaching: preparing to teach (research, lecture preparation, and logistical planning), teaching (performing classes and labs), and evaluation of that teaching (grading and entering grades). "Dealing with students" may seem like the largest component of being a professor, but students are usually either seeking help in the aftermath of teaching or seeking guidance regarding grades. Office hours and email responses still fit into the above categories. This list also includes something that might seem somewhat vague: thinking. However, our largest and most important job is to think—and then to disseminate that thinking to our students, colleagues, and those who read or respond to our publications. As a result, it is important that we reserve some time away from the madding crowd to stare out the window. Although some may scoff at the realism of this idea, Maggie Berg and Barbara K. Seeber, authors of *The Slow Professor*, assert that this is our top priority, and we need to make time for it. The list also includes "problems." It is obviously difficult to schedule problems and their aftermath into a daily schedule. However, we can set aside time either daily or weekly to deal with many of our problems. We don't have to have a knee-jerk reaction each time a problem arises.

The purpose of this exercise is to identify the times of day during which we are more energized and ready to do the activities on our lists. Many in our profession become night owls because they feel that the night hours give them more time and space to do work, unencumbered by family concerns or the pressures of the day. However, one of the most important suggestions in this book is to try—as much as possible—to become a "morning person." There are several good reasons to attempt this. Physiologically, we are fresher in the morning. Once we become accustomed to a morning routine, the beginning of the day has a freshness and energy that is hard to find at any other time. Second, traffic at gyms and on the road is often lightest in the early morning hours. Like night owls, early birds are often freed from responsibility (it is unlikely anyone will phone, stop by the office, or expect an email response at 6:30 a.m.). But the most important reason that morning is a perfect time for academics is that the weight of the day, the list of cares and concerns, is not weighing us down as it does at the end of the day. As much as we try to focus on work in the wee hours, we are still haunted by the pressures, the small or large frustrations, and the expectations others have placed on us throughout the day. Work done late at night is rarely as fresh and efficient because we simply have too much still on our minds. The morning allows not only a sense of repose but also a sense of possibility, as we have not yet faced the world.

However, if we are fully committed to working in the evenings, we should schedule our most important, laborious, and energy-consuming activities for that time. Of the list above, some things are less demanding than others. For example, posting readings to a course management system is rote and can be done when tired. Do not do these kinds of activities during most precious high-energy moments. Writing original prose is likely the most demanding task that we do in the academy, so the time of maximum energy and focus needs to be reserved for that task. Editing and reworking prose is probably the second-most difficult or demanding task and should take up the next prioritized block of time. For instance, perhaps academics find that morning is the best time for work, but it takes some time to "warm up," collect their thoughts, and be ready for new creation. In that case, they should use one of the early shoulders of the workday (perhaps 8:00–9:00 a.m.) to rework, edit, and think about their projects and start writing at 9:00 a.m. when their energy and focus are in full swing.

Most often we cannot control the times of the day or week when our classes are scheduled, but for very creative morning people, ask for late-day class times (often less desirable than midday classes) to provide a long stretch of writing or thinking before getting into teaching mode. Similarly, for those who write or think well at midday, when many people experience an energy surge, try to get the less popular early morning class time. Chairs appreciate evidence that their department members have put a lot of thought and energy into productivity; they may well be willing to work on course scheduling that makes the best of both teaching and research modes. By first getting clear on a mission, and then on ourselves, we can start to really harness the hours of the day and the things we should be doing at those times. To flesh these ideas out further, the next chapter deals specifically with time.

Chapter 2

Time

Of all the chapters of this book, academics may find themselves attracted to this one first. We would all like more time, particularly quality time—whether that is to write, to teach, to grade, or to enjoy our lives. Fortunately, there are ways to organize and plan schedules that will allow for more productivity and some leisure time at the end of the day. The first thing to remember about time is that it is finite; we all have the same amount in a day. No matter how rich, privileged, or blessed we are, we have the same number of hours per day as everyone else. What we have accomplished at the end of a day, or a life, is largely dependent on how we spend this resource. That's why it is critical that we learn to manage it well. To be fair, however, time itself is not the issue that needs to be addressed: instead, we need to understand energy and focus. No amount of time will be helpful if we don't have the mental or physical energy needed to accomplish tasks.

We can certainly organize our time and energy around the work before us; creating a mission (which we did in the previous chapter) may help us decide what the most important of those tasks are. However, it is also important to cut sideways across the swath of things we need to do or maintain, somewhere in between the details of the everyday and the larger question of why we are on the planet. Here, we get into roles and responsibilities, along with areas of focus. Stephen Covey writes quite a bit about how our roles and relationships to others help to define a well-lived life. These areas reflect responsibilities that we must meet. David Allen talks about "areas of focus," a similar concept. A list of roles might look something like this:

- Teacher
- Scholar
- Member of university community/department
- Parent
- Spouse
- Family member
- Friend
- Member of a service group or faith community
- Athlete
- Musician
- Home manager

Most people reading this book are both teachers and scholars, but we are also members of our university departments and communities, and we often have work to do in relation to those identities. Some academics are parents or spouses, most of us have family members outside of our immediate circle who require attention or support, and we all have friends. In addition, we often take on roles in the community and a religious group, and some of us may identify as musicians, athletes, pet owners, home managers, financial directors, and so on. When we are going through a weekly or monthly check of things to do, we should think about which of the roles we fulfill are most important and how we might best meet the expectations involved in those roles in the coming days.

An area of focus, similarly, represents some part of our life requiring maintenance or effort regardless of whatever other projects we have on the go. There are usually four or five subsets of focus within any particular role. For example, a parent might have an area of focus called "daughter."

This area could contain the following subsets:

School and education
Health
Sports and extracurricular activities
Social/friends
Clothes, gear, games, and apps

Each of these subcategories, in turn, contains lists of important tasks and not-to-be-missed deadlines.

Turning to the strictly academic life, each responsibility or role will also encompass areas of focus that take work and maintenance. Here are the areas of focus for the chair of a busy music department:

- Advancement/fundraising
- Curriculum/academic matters
- Recruitment
- Publicity/outreach
- Performance
- Departmental governance
- Administrative/organizational
- Relationship with university community
- Development/enrichment/staffing
- Academic advising/students
- University service
- Building management
- Special projects/initiatives

Each of these areas involves projects to be started or managed. So, for instance, under the first area, "Advancement/fundraising," are the following projects:

1. Alumni
    Alumni newsletters (three per year)
    Elliott Scholarship
2. "Friends of Department" project
3. Pep band equipment
4. Ensemble tours
5. Percussion renewal
6. Hall renovations
7. Computer lab refurbishment
8. Internal/external grants
9. Scholarships and in-course prizes

Each one of these was a discrete project, but simply having this list of projects and being able to look at it over once a week were helpful in staying on top of those tasks. David Allen organizes tasks according to projects, after advocating that we occasionally bump up to higher levels of generality before dipping down into the weeds to get individual tasks done. In fact, he suggests that we cannot "do" projects; we can only do next specific actions that move those projects forward. We may have on our to-do list an item such as "change winter tires." This item may have been lingering for quite some time, and the reason for this is that it involves multiple steps:

- Ask spouse when he/she needs the car this week
- Get number of a good mechanic from colleague
- Phone garage to make appointment
- Email spouse to communicate appointment time
- Bring winter tires up from the basement and put in car
- Go to garage and have the appointment
- Put summer tires in basement

In fact, only one of these tasks is possible at a time and probably only in this sequence. It is not possible to make an appointment if we do not know who we are calling for that appointment, for instance. Failure to identify the next step in any project is what will keep us stuck and unable to move forward.

Academic life is sometimes about being overwhelmed. The simple concept of "next actions" will calm the feeling of overwhelm. Here is how to break down the feeling of overwhelm and turn it into "calm control."

- Overwhelmed: Start of Term
  - Sense of Calm Control:
    Print off class list from web
    Check reserve list online on library site
    Draft email to students regarding Learning Management System
    Spend 10 minutes cleaning off desk for 2 days
    Shop for wine for departmental potluck
- Overwhelmed: Book
  - Sense of Calm Control:
    Highlight all library items relevant to chapter 2
    Order two library loan items online
    Write to Library of Congress regarding photo permission
    Copy manuscript submission criteria from University Press

As academics, we often look at tasks like "write book" as supremely overwhelming projects with so many moving parts that we do not know where to start. However, if we take some time to plan ahead and then break the project down into the smallest, most manageable chunks, we will be well on the way to its completion. In writing a book like this one, for instance, one could set a goal of writing 2,000 words a day, regardless of how one felt or how well-prepared one was to write. The natural next step would be to read over the section, send it to a research assistant (a colleague or friend could fill the same role) for a gut reaction, and then look at what has been written the day before. This method of creation followed by polishing of the previous section means that work can be built up in discrete units and then sewn together as a unified whole.

A RESEARCH DAY

As a consequence of going through the "best time of day" and "worst time of day" activities as advocated in the previous chapter, this is what a Research Day could look like:

- Wake up early, warm up the mind with some internet surfing, and take a cursory look at email
- Reread what was written yesterday, and edit it in 90-minute units organized according to Pomodoros (for an explanation of Pomodoros see the third chapter on "Writing")
- Take a longer break between three and four Pomodoros to clean up the kitchen and maybe put in a load of laundry
- Next, reread what was just written and consider it some more
- Make a to-do list, go out and run some errands, and do something physical
- Then two more stints of 90 minutes, capitalizing on a mid- to late-afternoon energy surge, doing some light housework in between Pomodoros
- Shower after the workday is over around 5:00 p.m., and then at night read material related to research—but no writing

This combination of some light, nonthinking work and a series of intense writing periods seems to work well for maintaining focus for most people. The time of day that different activities occur is dependent on one's personal rhythms and proclivities.

THE ACADEMIC YEAR

While the business world usually works in quarters according to a calendar year, with a fiscal year-end sometime in the winter, the academic year is unique to our field. Granted, "back to school," March break, and summer holidays often coincide with annual milestones in wider society. Still, our sense of timing has very specific purposes and parameters. For most schools, the academic year begins on July 1. This is usually the time when tenure-track hires start, collective agreement years begin, and tenure and promotion outcomes take effect.

July: For most of us, this is midsummer. July is the point by which all summer research and writing plans are reassessed. Many of us feel a sense of success or failure about our summer writing in July. Many of our research funds or other awards kick in and we can start purchasing materials we need for the fall. We reassess what the rest of the summer season will look like, measuring out goals and writing plans accordingly. For many, however, this is also the month for vacations, and many campuses are as quiet as they'll ever be.

August: At many institutions, teaching starts before Labor Day, and so August is the main time for teaching preparation, making sure teaching resources are up to date and functional and working out last-minute registration issues. We upload content to course management systems and have our first faculty meetings of the year. This is also a time when orientations for new faculty take place, orientation for students is ongoing, and placement tests for certain disciplines are written. For many, this is the time for last-ditch efforts to submit manuscripts and meet deadlines before the school year starts and, for others, a last opportunity to take some well-earned vacation before our time is dictated by others.

September: The headiest month of the year. Even seasoned professors can get butterflies leading up to those first days of class. Everything is fresh and new, classes are in full swing, and we are getting to know our students. Often this is a harried time, as research that we submitted in the summer months is coming back for review and editing just when everything else is gearing up: committees launch, university Senates start meeting to review rules and regulations, and there are beginning of year mixers with faculty, new students, or some combination of the two. We meet some of our new colleagues for the first time. We are filled with hope that this year our schedules, time, and energy will be different. September is a month of possibility.

October: October often includes a fall or (in places like Canada) a Thanksgiving break. This is the time of year when most of our problems start to surface: students who don't show up to class, our first midterms where we discover what did and did not work, and tenure and promotion hearings. We hunker down for the next few months and the work that they will bring. Grant applications are often due this month, so a lot of work may be needed to get those proposals ready for the following season. October is probably the hardest time to get writing and research done, and we should accept that this is just a natural part of the yearly cycle.

November: This is a month where our energy stores start to wane. We have been in full teaching mode for weeks and have faced our first plagiarism cases and sick days and (even worse) our partners or children have a fall cold. We and our families are deep into extracurricular activities, be they children's sports or our favorite yoga class. November includes the Thanksgiving break in the United States, and for many this is a time for family and perhaps a minor re-group. Some spend their holiday time grading or preparing for the last weeks of classes.

December: This is the month for grading. For most professors, final exams, assignments, and papers are due around this time, and they come in waves throughout the month. Holiday parties, concerts, and other social activities can dominate our time, while the outcomes of working committees or Senate activities come to a head. Curriculum that needs to go into an academic calendar or for a curricular review is seen around this time. We also are at our lowest point, physically and mentally, after the strenuous fall. We are ready for a break. Unfortunately, the writing we did in September or October is back for another round of revisions. Most schools run exam periods anywhere from the beginning of the month to just before Christmas break. For many academics, holidays are spent doing even more grading.

January: A new start. Breaks for Canadian schools offer only a week or two between final marks being submitted and the start of a new term. In the United States, there can be a fairly long intersession lasting three weeks before classes start. At this point in the year, many funding and granting deadlines come due. We have to start thinking, at least superficially, about our summer research plans. We definitely have to have our winter term courses in hand, something that does not necessarily take place during the previous summer's preparation. All our committee work, projects, and extracurriculars start up again, and we have a renewed sense of hope that this term things will be under better control and there will be more time. In keeping with New Year's resolutions, many of us vow to start or restart an exercise program, eat better, or get more sleep.

February: If granting cycles have not started in the fall months or January, they may well do so at this time. Plans for internships, summer research assistants, or summer research travel likely need to be cemented, and the usual midterms, assignments, and papers also come in for grading. For many schools, spring break takes place in February. While for many students it is a time for celebrating and heading south, for professors it is a brief chance to catch our breath and get some research or writing done. February has deadlines for academic changes to the curriculum and academic calendars. This is also the time when courses are entered into a timetable for the upcoming year. Some schools have preregistration for the fall term, so administrators and department heads can expect to spend the month timetabling, assigning workloads, and advising students on course selection.

March: March can be a nasty month. For those in cooler climates, the weather is often depressing. We have reached a point in the term when energy reserves plummet; the best-laid plans for more leisure time, an exercise routine, and advanced scheduling have gone by the wayside. We may be learning the outcome of granting cycles that change our summer plans. Grading and lecturing continue. It is hard to get as much done in March as we might hope, and this is when the majority of academic depression sets in.

April: Academics at some schools are wrapping up their courses and entering exams, grading final papers and tests, and starting to see the light at the end of the tunnel. (For American institutions, where classes tend to go late, April is the final stretch and the end comes in early May.) April need not be the proverbial cruelest month (March may still hold that title), but it can be a time when we start to look with hope toward the summer months and the prospect of more control over our time.

May: Freedom from a timetable is one of the benefits of this month. For Canadians, there are a few weeks between the end of submitting grades and spring graduation. This is when research time writ large really starts. For American schools, this break comes a little later but promises the same fulfillment. We make final plans for the summer, including research-related travel, childcare, and goals. We also contemplate a well-deserved vacation.

June: Many academics take June as their vacation time. For those lucky enough to have tenure-track or tenured positions, this is a time to re-group. It is also prime conference season, and many people are out on the road giving papers, seeing colleagues, and making deeper connections to their disciplines and their work. Spirits are high in May and June as the weather in most parts of North America is pleasant, we have no timetables, and our administrative work is mostly wrapped up for the year. In June, we can look forward to our highest levels of energy, focus, and relaxation. Life is good.

Of course, this time line works for universities with terms rather than semesters, so depending on what part of the world you call home, the outline of each month may change significantly. (Australians, for instance, may have snow while the rest of us enjoy summer weather.) However, we should consider our unique situations and imagine how the cycle of the year might work for us. How can we best take advantage of its rhythms? Mentally balance the periods of intense pressure with those of repose, plan ahead, and start imagining how to make the most of this cycle.

Here's a sample general year plan with focus points in each month as discretionary work:

MONTHLY SCHEDULE

July Holiday
Train athletically
Retreat (three days)

August Class preparation: read all textbooks, revise class plans, and hand in course reserves
Train athletically
Revisions to research and finalization
Mini-break before school starts
Take weekends off

September	Class preparation: finalize details on syllabus and make copies
	Reading/studying for courses/listening
	Present research publicly
	Socializing—yearly party
	Finish grant applications in first two weeks
	Compete in 5K
October	Research: revisions
	Funding reports
	New research: books in own library
	Mini-break on the 15th
November	Research: Interlibrary loan material
	Revisions if necessary
	Cooking
	Last two weeks—fitness maintenance only in preparation for athletic training
	Finalize next term courses
	Prepare exams and evaluations
	Aesthetics and massage before end of classes
December	Research: writing
	Train athletically
	Paper proposals for following year based on research
	Mini-break at the 1st of month
January	Funding applications (research): internal
	Projects for summer planned
	Socializing
February	Taxes
	Redo filing system
	Finish funding applications begun in January
	Fitness maintenance—one or two weeks
	Retreat four days or intensive writing and research
March	Class planning, following year, and preliminary courses
	Prepare exams and course evaluations
	Self-reading and relaxation
	Aesthetics and massage before end of classes
	Cooking
April	Clean out house, dry cleaning, and clothing inventory
	Grant application preparation for fall
	Class planning for following year and detailed syllabus

May	Plan research trips Mini-break at the 1st of month Start taking weekends off Class planning, finish syllabus, and order textbooks—have readers printed Fitness maintenance—one or two weeks to prepare for athletic training Research—reading and preliminary writing Mini-break on the 15th Set up dates to present research in first few weeks of September Newsletter update and Faculty Activity Report
June	Research: writing Train athletically Take weekends off

A note about this schedule: the work assigned to different months relates fairly closely to the above schedule of the year. Physical activity is important, but some parts of the school year make it harder to maintain a fitness regimen, especially compared to the summer. "Training athletically" is easier during months with more free time and requires advance preparation. "Cooking" is a priority during particularly harried months when we are likely to let nutrition slip. Note that self-care routines like aesthetics, massage, and home-based cooking are also prioritized during the tough months. These activities provide not only things to anticipate with pleasure but also ways to stay healthy and energized. Mini-retreats (more on this in the "Life" chapter) are meant as opportunities to recharge. Make sure plans for the year are realistic when balancing work, life, and avocation. It is also worth remembering when certain conferences usually take place so that we can plan travel, research, writing, and home life around them. In the summer, one option is to take weekends off work. This is a valuable lesson about academic life that we often forget: we don't have to be all out all year long. Let the seasonal changes allow for a breather every now and then. Although putting together a monthly plan like this can be very helpful to get the big picture, the rubber really hits the road on a weekly or daily basis. This means that we need to start at the micro level because it is there that the most impactful decisions really take place.

The Academic Week

Most professors teach on a Monday-to-Friday schedule. Although some teach in the evenings, in the weekends, or—more usually in the summer months—on a compressed daily schedule, for most of us the rhythms of the days and weeks are generally fixed. Classes usually start no earlier than 8:00 a.m., and the last classes of the day finish no later than 5:30 p.m. or 6:00 p.m. Anything that goes much later into the evening can probably be considered a "night class."

Within this Monday-to-Friday schedule, most courses are given in blocks either on Mondays/Wednesdays/Fridays or on Tuesdays/Thursdays. At first, we might think it is efficient to arrange our classes on one or the other of those options, leaving the other days to do research and course preparation. However, this is not always as good a choice as it seems. Long stretches of uninterrupted time are necessary for our best work but not 12 hours at a time. Academic work, as we have seen, is best done in shorter intense bouts and not long stretches that lend themselves to email checking or other "release" activities not conducive to our goals. We also have to think about those poor department chairs—and our students—for whom course scheduling affects pedagogical efficacy. Demanding particular teaching times or days may seem convenient to us, but it is a nightmare for others and usually not worth it for anyone.

Although we will talk about how to schedule a full day of research, service, and teaching, let us first think about the block week as the best time frame to plan. Although we should think about research and teaching every day, and do something daily toward those areas, "themed days" are often the best way to focus on particular tasks. The thinking behind this is that we want to focus in deep work mode on particular projects, but it is also unrealistic to think that our days can be entirely devoted to that one task or project. Thinking this way sets us up for failure. Below is a typical example of themed days, a system that has worked very well for many academics.

Mondays: "Getting Things Done Day." On this day, catch up on all email and lingering projects from the week before, usually administrative tasks. There is a logic to this. Most people think about what they are concerned about, or want help with, over the weekend. For academics who work weekends (and that is most of us), firing off numerous emails on a Sunday night or Monday morning is quite a common way to jump-start the week. We have had time to ruminate over our academic life, and this often results in a flurry of communications. Email inboxes are busier on a Monday morning than at any other time. It is also a high-volume time for people to make medical appointments, call service providers, and cross off other chores on their to-do list, which is why call volumes tend to peak on Mondays. We should still work on our most important tasks, and make time for writing and teaching, but Monday is a good day to power through the inbox and clean everything up. The other benefit to Mondays is that we are fresh; the exhausting aspect of some of this email cleanup or attention to administrative tasks is better tackled when we are in a better mood and have more energy.

Tuesdays: "Teaching Day." This day can come on any day of the week, unlike Monday, which is a particularly good time for grinding through quotidian or unpleasant tasks. Teaching preparation for the week can be done in one day if we are focused, mindful, and in teaching mode. But Teaching Day is not just a day to get caught up on grading or do last-minute course preparation. It is a day to think deeply about our teaching, our pedagogy, and projects we would like to develop. Interested in creating a new course or curriculum? Set aside some time on this day to think and plan. Take some of this focused work time and sketch out the new course, curricular, or pedagogical idea. By focusing on teaching specifically on this day, we create a "retreat" environment in which we can get more done with less distraction. Work on the scholarship of teaching and learning is best done on Teaching Day. Again, actual teaching and writing (and perhaps meetings) will occur on this day, but the major focus—the mindset of the day—is around teaching. This is also an excellent day to hold office hours, be they electronic or physical. Focusing on students will keep us in the right frame of mind, and we will do our best work for them on Teaching Day.

Wednesdays: "Administrative Day" or "People Day." Many people with a Monday/Wednesday/Friday schedule will have a lot of teaching to do on Wednesday. So Wednesdays can become the "long day at school." This could be any other day of the week and, like Teaching Day, depends entirely on when most other commitments fall. However, Administrative Day is a good day to have meetings and do the work that the university expects us to do on their behalf. This may be the one day when we do less writing, but as long as we can spend some dedicated time at least reading or reflecting on our research, that time will be well worth it. Trying to see everyone in one day seems like it would be exhausting. Surprisingly, People Day can become an energized and enjoyable day of the week. We thrive on human contact; knowing we can put off everything but our interactions with people for an entire day a week is very freeing.

Thursdays: "Research Preparation Day." Research and writing academic prose are the most time-, energy-, and focus-consuming tasks in academic life. As a result, care must be taken in preparing for research and writing so that they take place as effortlessly as possible. Although some time each day should be spent working on our research programs, writing, and editing a little, Thursday and Friday are the days when we are most likely to get this done. For one thing, Thursday is usually not a loaded Teaching Day (except for those of us with heavy Tuesday/Thursday classes). Research preparation, then, like all advanced preparation, can take place when most of the rush of the week is over. Preparation involves planning our writing and research time. There is nothing worse than opening a new document and preparing to work when we have not planned what we will write, what sources we will use, what part of the project we will attack, or where our resources can be found. Thursday allows us to prepare the bibliography, put sources in order, review where we last left our project, or pick up items that we may need to consult. Without this preparation, we are likely to waste at least an hour getting ready to work—either collecting our thoughts or collecting necessary materials. Research preparation also involves rereading what we have written during the past week and reflecting on what we want to do next. Some gentle editing of earlier prose is a great way to get our minds completely back up and running in writing mode. If we have family commitments or other activities that occur on Thursday nights, we should ask for a few hours alone to do research preparation.

Fridays: "Research Day." One might think that Friday is the worst day to focus on research, but ironically, it can often be the best. First, most of the rush of the week is over. Most people in the university have become so bogged down in their own work and commitments that they are no longer emailing or stopping by the office. Students have started to wind down for the weekend's social activities and are less likely to need office hour appointments or support. The day leads naturally into a weekend where reflection can take place. If Friday is not an all-out meeting or Teaching Day, consider setting aside several hours—as many as possible—for concentrated research and writing. The other benefit to using Fridays as Research Days is that we are tired, meaning that our subconscious minds don't batter us with imposter syndrome or guilt, shame, and fear about what we have or have not done. A little fatigue releases some of these common but unhelpful perfectionist qualities, and knowing that a restorative weekend is coming up prompts us to work. In David Allen's *Getting Things Done* methodology, we reserve an hour or two a week for a Weekly Review of projects and action items. In addition to some good writing and thinking time, the Weekly Review fits very well on a Friday. Leave the office organized and in good shape; spend an hour reflecting on administrative and other university commitments. This will create a list of emails to send, letters to write, and errands to run that can all be done on Monday.

Saturdays: "Rest Day." Although it flies in the face of all our academic conditioning, it is important to take off one day a week. Two is even better, if possible. There are many benefits to resting. For one thing, we are not machines. We cannot grade, read, and write seven days a week. This leads to burnout; one of the most important things we have to learn in the thirteen- or fourteen-week term is to pace ourselves. One extremely productive academic decided to take a Sabbath. Sundays were her designated day, as she also had a religious observance on this day. She did no academic work all day. "This is the most powerful thing I've ever done, and I work so much better and more efficiently when I do it," she said. The psychology is fairly basic: time to regenerate mind, body, and spirit is essential to leading a balanced life. We need to recharge our batteries in order to do our very difficult and demanding jobs. Whether we decide to take our rest day on Saturday or Sunday, it is a day to play. Spend time with family and friends, cook, shop, take a day trip, and even go to bed early. We deserve this time and we have earned it.

Sundays: "Day of Recreation." We may want to take this as one of our days off. It makes sense: some people have a religious observance on Sundays, and they are traditionally considered a day for family. However, consider using Sunday for a special kind of preparation called "recreation." Recreation involves long-range planning or what Covey would call Type II activities. Some academics enjoy doing their Weekly Review on a Sunday, as it is a quieter day with time to think deeply about projects and time lines. Sundays also lend themselves to workouts or yoga, meal preparation for the week, and deep dives into mission or long-range thinking. One option is to use the day for lunch and breakfast preps for the week, along with planning nonacademic weekly activities. It is a day to do some nonessential reading, meditate, and spend time with others. It can also be used as a catchup day for things that have not gotten the attention they deserve during the week. However the day is used, it should focus on formative thinking and planning, so that one feels truly "re-created" and ready to face the busyness of Mondays. Of course, if we do not work on a Monday-to-Friday schedule, the suggestions for Saturday and Sunday may not apply. They are just that—suggestions for how to make these days relaxing and fulfilling both for our personal lives and our academic roles.

The themed days approach works well for several reasons: we cannot write, teach, or do research for an entire twelve-hour day. But we spend a given day focusing carefully on one or two activities, allowing us to harness the two essentials to academic life: energy and focus.

Daily Schedules

Whether or not we use themed days, we must consider the landscape of each day in our week. This is where the very important daily scheduling comes in. The "Know Thyself" exercise in the first chapter, which indicates the best time to do certain tasks, is essential to daily scheduling. David Allen teaches that what we do at any given time is dependent on three variables: time, energy, and context. Figuring out our best physical locations, time windows, and what we do best at different times of the day will help to create a great daily plan. There is no point starting an important writing exercise with 10 minutes between classes. This might be a good time, however, to make a few quick phone calls or file some lecture notes. Be smart about windows of time. Figure 2.1 shows a typical daily schedule.

Research: 12 hours, 33 percent   Upper Body: 2 hours, 9 minutes
Teaching: 20 hours, 56 percent   Back and Abs: 2 hours, 1 minute
Administration: 4 hours, 11 percent   Lower Body: 2 hours, 17 minutes

It is worth calculating how long we spend on teaching, research, and service. No one can balance these perfectly all year; however, getting a sense of how much time we are spending on each area will be helpful in figuring out how our priorities work. In the schedule above, note that there is some teaching and research on each day, but it is easy to theme these days according to the system discussed earlier. It is important to

SCHEDULE – WINTER TERM

	MONDAY	TUESDAY	WEDNESDAY	THURSDAY	FRIDAY	SATURDAY	SUNDAY
7:00 – 8:00	Morning Prayer	Morning Prayer	Morning Prayer	Morning Prayer	Morning Prayer		
8:00 – 9:00	Prep 20th C.	Office Hours & Class Prep	Prep 20th C.	Email & Prep	Prep 20th C.	Week Planning	
9:00 – 10:00	MUSC 3251		MUSC 3241	Gym	MUSC 3241	Run	
10:00 – 11:00		Administration					Prep for Church
11:00 – 12:00	Prep 2201		Prep 2201	Shower & Commute	Prep 2201	Gym	
12:00 – 1:00	MUSC 2201	Lunch	MUSC 2201	Lunch	MUSC 2201		Church
1:00 – 2:00	Lunch & Email		Department Meeting	Research	Commute/Lunch		Lunch
2:00 – 3:00	Administration		Office Hours		Research, Errands		Gym
3:00 – 4:00	Gym	Gym	Collegium or Errands				
4:00 – 5:00	Snack	Snack	Commute	Commute	Commute		
5:00 – 6:00	Evening Prayer & Commute	Evening Prayer & Commute	Evening Prayer & Commute	Evening Prayer & Commute	Evening Prayer & Commute		
6:00 – 7:00	Dinner	Dinner	Dinner	Dinner	Dinner		
7:00 – 8:00	Research	Research	Eucharist	Research	Free		
8:00 – 9:00			Free Time		Free		
9:00 – 10:00	Yoga	Yoga	Bed	Yoga	Free		

Figure 2.1 Weekly Schedule.

schedule in nonacademic commitments, like the daily religious observance that took place in an actual place of worship. Also consider commute times and the number of hours it takes to do different workouts. This example gives an idea of how long it would take to go through various workout scenarios.

The secret to daily scheduling is to understand two things: one, people or things will interrupt the schedule, and, two, this should not be an excuse to give up on having a schedule. We can always get back on track, or at least approximate our schedule, if we have interruptions to scheduled tasks. Mapping out things like exercise and writing time will be vital to meeting our goals and maintaining our life balance. We need to be gentle with ourselves when we—inevitably—cannot be perfect every day. As long as we can analyze our time over the week as is laid out above, we will find that we can fit in time for those work or life activities that will give us the balance we need.

In the academic world, we devote a certain percentage of our time to different aspects of our roles: teaching, research, and service. In a typical university, which has a 2+3 load (meaning that we teach two courses in one term and three in the other), the allocation works out to roughly

- 40 percent research
- 40 percent teaching
- 20 percent service(a 1+1 load would make for 80 percent research)

If we consider the time we spend teaching, grading, and attending to service responsibilities, as well as the number of pure Research Days in a term, we may come up with a different calculation depending on discipline-based or departmental activities. This is a sobering thought. Ninety days at 40 hours per week is not a lot of time to do the necessary concentrated work, plus clean up from the previous term. This is especially true in the summer, when we are unlikely to work 40 hours a week. The breakdown of teaching, research, and service also fluctuates throughout the year. We probably do complete the 20 percent service during the school year, spend significantly more time teaching during term, and do most of our research in the spring and summer months. It is not unwise, then, once we have completed a weekly schedule to calculate how much time we are spending on each of these roles to ensure we are allocating enough energy and focus to maintain a balance. It is also important, when thinking about service, to balance the service we do for outside organizations, like disciplinary societies, with the service we do within the university. It is easy to get overwhelmed by taking on too much in these roles. And, for pre-tenure faculty, it is especially important not to get overcommitted to activities that will not help our promotion case.

Many academics find that in their senior years, when most of their courses are under control and they have achieved tenure and promotion, they spend more time on university service, especially in areas like curriculum development, governance, and reviewing grant and tenure applications. This is a normal part of the life cycle of the university career. In assessing how much time to devote to the three pillars of teaching, research, and service, we should consider where we are on this spectrum and what is appropriate for our season of life. After doing the mission work earlier in this volume, "knowing thyself" in terms of energy cycles of the day, and considering the academic year and themed days, we should be well on the way to figuring out how to use our time to give us the best schedule we can. This is not easy, and it often takes months or years to work out, but it is well worth the effort if it results in a more productive and stress-free academic life.

Chapter 3

Writing

A key to advanced planning is to be realistic about what one can accomplish. Most academics are caught in a cycle where they say "yes" to everything and then find themselves crunched for time and facing horrendous deadlines or getting behind in their regular work. Extending deadlines for academic research has become so normal that presses and journals simply accept it. But wouldn't it be nice to work ahead of a deadline, polishing and finishing up the last details a few days in advance without tearing our hair out or pulling all-nighters? It's possible with some serious advanced planning but only when we are realistic about our goals. A humanities article recently won an excellence award from its disciplinary society and was published in a major first-tier journal. When asked, the author confirmed that he had initially written a longer version that was eventually cut down into two articles. It took him months during a leave to write the longer article, and he had been working through the ideas behind it since graduate school, probably thirty years before the article went to press.

We don't all need to constantly publish such long, award-winning articles in first-tier journals, but this should give us an idea of how long it really takes to do good academic work—and what is the point of aiming for less? Consider the average academic humanities publication and how many hours it takes to research, write, and edit. (Scientific publications are shorter and more frequent, so the time line may vary for academics in the sciences.) Then imagine, with a full-time teaching job, plus sabbaticals or leaves, how long it would really take someone to produce this work. When facing tenure and promotion, and depending on the expectations of each university, we are pushed to publish as much as possible, as fast as possible. However, one well-placed publication in a major journal is worth more than numerous "smallest publishable units" on lesser platforms. We should think carefully and strategically about the work we produce, especially as it relates to the stage of our careers.

Once we have determined how long it will take to do the work, we should think carefully about our program of research. Much like a teaching philosophy, a research program is often written for promotion or job applications. However, like a good mission statement, it should be updated and ready to go at all times, because it provides the blueprint for what we hope to achieve—and why. Before determining what must be done in the coming months and years, we should write a research statement clearly identifying the major issues we would like to address in our work over a three-to-five-year period. Ultimately, so many things change in our lives as academics that there is no point in planning beyond three years, or, at the most, five. Different projects, competing schedules and opportunities, health issues, family concerns, funding, and teaching responsibilities can all change our course. Realistic goals are key if we want to set ourselves for success.

When planning academic projects, then, we should think along several lines at once:

1. Books or monographs published or edited
2. Journal articles published
3. Papers read at conferences
4. Special events or projects
5. Teaching
6. Committee work
7. Professional development
8. Funding (and funding applications)
9. Leaves or promotions

Remember that summers will be the primary time for concentrated work on academic projects and that we should expect to accomplish less during the teaching year. The best way to do this initial planning is with a chart called a "Career Itinerary." Figure 3.1 gives an example for the years 2017–2020.

RESEARCH & TEACHING: CAREER ITINERARY

Academic Year	Summer 2017	2017/2018	Summer 2018	2018/2019	Summer 2019	2019/2020	Summer 2020	2020/2021
Papers	LB and the Beatles for Hong Kong	Colorado Paper Kansas Papers	RMA Conference	Mt. A: RMA Conference AMS: Washington Panel Skidmore Paper	Work on Gypsy paper	Regional conference: Gypsy Paper		AMS: Gypsy paper Mt. A. Colloquium: Gypsy paper
Publications		Work on JAMS Article: Jewish West Side Story 1 Book Review	JAMS Article: Jewish West Side Story LB and the Beatles for Echo Studies in Musical Theatre on Angry YM	Work on Gypsy; 1 Book Review	Archival work on Gypsy	1 Book Review Gypsy Article		
Special Events/Projects		Musical Theatre textbook	Musical Theatre textbook	LB Centennial in Rochester Jamie Crooks artist in-residency	Musical Theatre Textbook	Musical Theatre Textbook		
SoTL	1) STLHE. Compassionate Classroom 2) STLHE. IFNTF Session	JMHPED: Signature Pedagogies in Musicology	STLHE: Time Management STLHE: Internship with B. JMHPED: Signature Pedagogies in Musicology Signature Pedagogies with Jessica	AAU Teaching Showcase: Pedagogy Course	STLHE: The Role of the Dean in promoting teaching and learning	AAU Teaching Showcase: The Role of the Dean in promoting teaching and learning		AAU Teaching Showcase: something with Toni?
Teaching		Musical Theatre		Pedagogy Course or Beatles	Revamp Research Methods	Research Methods		
Professional Development	Micro-Doctoral Certificate course			Sabbatical				

Figure 3.1 Career Itinerary.

This document can be created in Word or Excel and is easy to edit as needed. Consider the balance between categories. Do you have a big conference to organize? Less writing will get done. Are you on too many committees or have too many new courses to prepare? Consider renegotiating some of those agreements. Looking down the columns shows commitments and gets a sense of whether they are balanced (or not). Horizontally, the itinerary traces the development of a project from research to writing to publishing. We can also work on a few smaller projects with a monograph bubbling away on another mental burner.

The itinerary can and should be used for tenure and promotion dossiers as well as in mentoring colleagues. However, the itinerary is not just useful for demonstrating planning to others. It is also a powerful way to remind ourselves of what we can and cannot do with our limited time. This allows us to say no to any projects that do not fit our time lines. We also have the choice to rewrite our time lines when something irresistible comes along. The document should be printed and posted in the workspace as a reminder to always stay on track.

Of course, the Career Itinerary can be expanded to a whole-life itinerary. One option is to spread the chart onto a second page and include leaves, administrative goals, and hobbies. When reading vertically, that provides an even better sense of whether there is too much on our plates. If family planning is in the cards, this chart is very helpful for imagining when parental leave might best take place. The great thing about the Career Itinerary is that it forces us to recognize that we cannot do everything we want to and that this is okay. We all take on too much and then find that we cannot meet our commitments on time or in the way we would like. The Career Itinerary not only facilitates the advanced planning that results in great finished projects but also balances the time we spend in different areas of our work lives.

A corollary to the Career Itinerary is the Planning Document. This should be written around the same time as the Career Itinerary. Use it to lay out important dates, deadlines, time lines, budgets, and so on, for all projects so that they can all be visualized at once. It is best to use a header on the electronic document that indicates what it is, where it is stored on the computer, and when it was last updated. Here is a sample document for an administrative leave.

PRELIMINARY PLANNING

I. General Information and Scheduling

Dates: July 1, 2018–August 31, 2019
Vacation: July 9–13, 2018, December 16–21, 2018
Important Dates and Meetings

1. January 1, 2019: Admin leave begins
2. February 15, 2019: Bell Fund application due
3. March 1, 2019: Research Committee applications due
4. June 30, 2019: Admin leave ends
5. August 30, 2019: Back to school
6. October 15, 2019: National Insight Grant application due

II. Major Scholarly Projects

1. Musical Theatre textbook: Prospectus and sample chapter
2. One book review for one journal: January
3. Jewish *West Side Story*
4. Angry Young Men for *Studies in Musical Theatre*
5. Bernstein In Context book proposal
6. Cambridge Companion to *West Side Story*
7. Branden paper on Bernstein
8. Proceedings from AAU Showcase
9. Signature Pedagogies workshop
10. Threshold Concepts in Music History
11. Bonn Bernstein Conference
12. *The Organized Academic* for publication
13. National Insight Grant application

III. Major Teaching and Career Projects

1. Job talks for job interviews
2. Signature Pedagogies and Renewal of Liberal Education

IV. Major Personal Projects

1. Achieve target weight
2. Bodybuilding training and getting more fit
3. Healing of athletic injuries
4. Friend's birthday trip
5. Sommelier course
6. Math studies

V. Research Expenses

1. Research assistant
2. 30 hours × 4 weeks

VI. Speaking Engagements and Papers

1. Mt. A. on Bernstein in January
2. Compassionate Classroom March in Brandon

VII. Time Line

January: Latouche, Bernstein Paper with Branden, Proceedings, Cambridge proposals, Bonn
February: Angry Young Men, *The Organized Academic*, Jewish article
March: Jewish article, *The Organized Academic*
April: Jewish article, *The Organized Academic*
May: Threshold Concepts, Signature Pedagogies, *The Organized Academic*
June: Vacation—Chicago? *The Organized Academic*
July: Bonn paper, course preparation
August: Course preparation

VIII. Weekly Schedule

1. Mondays: *The Organized Academic*, book review
2. Tuesdays: *The Organized Academic*, immediate stuff
3. Wednesdays: Bernstein entirely
4. Thursdays: Planning of research time, admin

IX. Daily Schedule

6 hours of musicology
1 hour of admin work on Thursdays
Fridays off and weekends off

PROJECT PLANNING

Textbook

1. Write to Natalie
2. Fill out form for textbook
3. Fill out other form for textbook
4. Read other textbooks

Latouche Review

1. Awaiting response

Jewish Article

1. Print notes from computer from last time
2. Read *Funny, It Doesn't Sound Jewish* by Gottlieb
3. Reread Most's dissertation and book
4. Read Most's other new book on liberalism
5. Read Lovensheimer

Angry Young Men for *Studies in Musical Theatre*

1. Awaiting response from editors

Bernstein in Context Proposal

1. Awaiting response from Kate

Cambridge Companion to *West Side Story*

1. Awaiting contract

Branden Paper on Bernstein

1. Need to submit to another conference
2. Need to submit to Memorial University

Proceedings from Atlantic Showcase

1. Awaiting response

Signature Pedagogies Workshop

1. Read the original Signature Pedagogies article
2. Read the other Signature Pedagogies book
3. Come up with what the Engaged Citizen looks like
4. Map out the qualities of the Engaged Citizen
5. Develop bibliography
6. Finish reading the other Signature Pedagogies book

Threshold Concepts in Music History

1. *Deep Work* thinking retreat
2. Make sure no one has done it in Music History yet—pedagogy journal
3. Do a database search
4. Read some other threshold concept books

Bernstein Conference January 2019

1. Report
2. Reimbursements

Get to Target Weight

1. Meal plan for next week
2. Gym visit Saturday
3. Tread climber once a week
4. Yoga daily

Branden Burry Commission

1. Find website information on grants
2. Waiting on Alex
3. Conference call

Emin Project

1. Phone call brainstorm

National Insight Grant

1. Have Kaye read Insight Grant proposal guidelines
2. Read yourself Insight Grant proposal guidelines
3. Have Kaye input CV into Common CV

    We all have many different projects on the go. This example included health goals and reading a whole raft of textbooks in preparation for proposing one. The necessary steps are listed as "next actions." When doing our planning at the beginning of the week, Planning Documents allow us to see what needs to be accomplished, on which project, and when. These documents are also a great place to do some budget calculations so that we know what we have to spend and what we need to ask for in funding applications. We should start this Planning Document about six months to a year out from when we plan to start the activities, so that, as different things come up, we can add them. Looking at it once a week to see where we are and what should take up our attention can be part of our Weekly Review. It will also allow us to update sections so that we remember when we are waiting for certain responses from others, and so on.

    There are many excellent books on how to write well and efficiently, everything from *The Clockwork Muse* by Eviatar Zerubavel to W. Brad Johnson and Carol A. Mullen's *Write to the Top!* There is no point in summarizing or rehashing the content of these sources, as they deserve their own read. But one thing all writing books emphasize is consistency in writing. Writing is like any practice, be it meditation or fitness. Regularity and consistency are the keys to ensuring things work smoothly and keeping us in good form. If we have put together a daily or weekly schedule like those presented in the previous chapter, we will be well on our way to carving out the time we need to write. However, there are some truly revolutionary techniques to improve our writing practices and keep us on track.

THE POMODORO TECHNIQUE

One of the practices that has transformed the daily work experience of many academics is the Pomodoro Technique invented by the Italian writer Francesco Cirillo in the late 1980s. Experimenting with time frames of attention and lack thereof, Cirillo came up with the ingenious idea of using a kitchen timer (his timer was shaped like a tomato or *pomodoro* in Italian). He set his timer for 25 minutes and devoted all of his attention to the task at hand until the timer went off. When it did, he took a 5-minute break and then started the timer again for another 25-minute stint. To read all about the technique, which also includes tracking and assessing the work done within each work block, check out https://francescocirillo.com/pages/pomodoro-technique.

The concept is very simple, but it is amazingly effective. When faced with a distracting world, the Pomodoro Technique sets aside a manageable stretch of time to be completely focused on one task, with the knowledge that a restorative break is right around the corner. No email, no phone calls, and no interruptions are allowed during the Pomodoro. And, more importantly, when the timer goes off to signal a break, that break must be taken. Admittedly, the break is not long enough to get anything else done, but that's the whole point. One simply needs to look up from the task, get a glass of water, or walk around for a few minutes, and then get right back at it. The break is not meant for checking email or doing other work on the computer; that would not really constitute a break. However, it is long enough to refresh the mind and keep it energized until the task is resumed.

The next step is to measure out any given task by how many Pomodoros it takes to complete. Cirillo advises that if a task will take more than three or four such stints, it should be broken up into different projects. That way, a sense of overwhelm does not set in. The Pomodoro Technique suggests that the traditional belief that work blocks should be 90 minutes long is too generous. It seems that anything over 90 minutes is too long: our attention and focus gradually fade so that we no longer are working at full capacity. What the Pomodoro Technique promises, and delivers, is that after every 25 minutes, the 5-minute break gets us right back up to our original level of full focus. Therefore, after 90 minutes chunked into three Pomodoros, we are as fresh as we were at the start. After four Pomodoros, one generally takes a longer break, perhaps 30 minutes or so. Although this might seem like a waste of time, the technique actually saves time in the long run because of the amount of focused work that can be accomplished in each Pomodoro.

The Pomodoro Technique has been used in business, but it has caught on like wildfire among the academic community, and this is no surprise. It can be used for everything from academic work to decluttering the garage and most find that it makes time go by quickly with maximum enjoyment and focus. Although Cirillo's full program of tracking and assessing the efficacy of the day's Pomodoros takes a little more time to implement, one can pick up the basics of this system instantly with whatever timer is at hand. Once we adopt the system, it is simply a matter of looking at the day ahead and determining how many Pomodoros we have available to us. Fourteen Pomodoros is not too many, and some of us have enough scheduling flexibility to fit that many into a day between other commitments. We should then plan out how many Pomodoros we predict it will take to accomplish each task. Once that is done, we get to work. It is amazing how many tasks can get done in a day using this system, especially tasks like writing reports or nonacademic writing, the kind of work that we tend to put off. If it would only take one Pomodoro to execute, it is worth it to try this system. One can buy online timers in the shape of tomatoes that are automatically set for 25 minutes and 5-minute breaks or download free apps. The other option is to go old-school and actually set a timer on a phone or kitchen device.

A ROOM OF ONE'S OWN

One of the most important components of being organized and in control of our academic lives is having space that is appropriate to our needs. Ideally, we would have both a home and a work office. However, if the plan is to do our academic work during normal business hours and at our university offices, we will not need a full setup at home. For many people it is hard to write at school. There are too many distractions and interruptions, the school office is not very physically comfortable, or research materials are so voluminous that they will not fit in one office. Therefore, consider using the school office for course preparation, with general materials and sources on hand, and creating a home study with research materials, a printer, and a home computer. If you are fortunate enough to have two laptops, use one for research and personal content and the other as a "school" computer for checking email and keeping course materials and administrative documents.

Regardless of whether working with one or two spaces, they need to be functional and free from clutter. It is very easy, in our paper-dense world, to accumulate detritus that we really do not need and that weighs us down physically and mentally. Make an attempt at the end or beginning of each school year to set aside one day to declutter your space. Have recycling and garbage cans nearby, and perhaps even hire a student to help with other physical clutter like extra copies of course textbooks that tend to accumulate on office shelves. Although much of our work is now done on computers, we have not entered a paperless society and will find that our attention and focus are much more reliable when we are not distracted by paper clutter. The same is true of a home office, whether we are lucky enough to have a full study or a space that we have carved out under a staircase or in a closet.

The coffee shop or similar public locations are also good places to work. There is something comforting in being around strangers and hearing a low hum of white noise; for some, the combination creates an ideal work environment. Public libraries are excellent places for academic work and most campuses will have smaller libraries or archives where there are fewer people to distract us from focused work. Seek out these spaces and claim one. The only rules are that (a) people cannot find you there and (b) you have enough space to spread out whatever research or teaching materials necessary to produce your best work. Even a space as innocuous as an atrium with waterfall in an office building can be an excellent place to get work done. Spend some time scoping out such places close to home or the office. The reward will be intense and distraction-free productivity.

Our workspaces should only contain the things that are necessary for productivity. Artwork and photos are fine, as well as essential tools like a scanner, printer, and essential office supplies. However, avoid the pitfall of piling up stacks of reading material to get to or papers to grade. These will be distracting on both a moral and visual level, as we'll feel guilty staring at the work still left to do (and who can say they have done everything they need to do?).

If working on a laptop with the capacity for docking, working on two screens can be very helpful. Most laptops come with docks, and screens do not have to be IMAX theater-sized to give us a good sense of what we are looking at. With two screens, we can work simultaneously on two parts of a document (for instance, a writing screen and a bibliography screen) or on two separate documents. It is also sometimes handy, especially when processing email or otherwise interacting with the outside world, to have a calendar or email on one screen and a task on the other. This should not be taken as an invitation to multitask, as multitasking is the attractive yet deadly enemy of the organized and productive academic.

Avoid having a cluttered bulletin board. It is very easy for meaningless things to accumulate on this surface and eventually we become blind to whatever meaning they once had. Be ruthless with this space. A calendar and frequently called numbers or account numbers would be helpful here (anything that would prevent having to look them up repeatedly).

It is also important to find a way to time activities, whether with a desktop tool or a physical timer. If working in Pomodoros, we must strictly time these segments of activity and the intervening breaks. If motivation or focus is hard to come by, we can try to apply ourselves for 10 minutes on a timer to see if the creative juices start flowing. Starting is no doubt the most difficult part of any writing or research assignment, but anyone can commit to doing 10 minutes, and it is amazing how quickly this can become several hours of productive work.

There are as many ways of arranging an academic workspace as there are people; however, to be inspired and impressed, visit the excellent site www.unclutterer.com. Not only does this site post interesting short pieces on organization and productivity (and advocate for an uncluttered environment), but it also has a special section featuring "ideal offices," often masterpieces of design and minimalism. We would all do well to reduce the amount of "stuff" in our office environments while following the lead and design ideas of these ideal workspaces. For graduate students, those low on cash, or anyone who doesn't have a lot of space or patience for fancy office setups, an effective home office can be made from two matching two-drawer filing cabinets topped by a plain hardware store door with a hole for a doorknob. Simply set the door on top of the filing cabinets, feed any wires or cords for electronics through the doorknob hole in the back, and—voilà!—a home office on a very small budget. There will be plenty of room to spread out all necessary materials and equipment and places to store physical paper in the filing cabinets.

Office chairs should take up most of any office furnishing budget. A chair with proper support, arms, and a comfortable amount of padding will allow us to work for longer, with less discomfort, and will make the work area more appealing. If uncomfortable at work, we should ask our administration for an ergonomic assessment. One professor was crippled with frozen shoulder until she realized that a move to a new office had meant a small adjustment to the angle of her keyboard. Fixing this problem through an ergonomic assessment resulted in a complete recovery and a more comfortable working environment. Above all, avoid the "secretary chair"—the cheapest of office chairs with no supportive back and no arms. It will cut into productivity because anyone who sits in it will constantly have to adjust it or escape from its confines.

INTER LIBRARY LOAN AND RESEARCH ASSISTANTS

Inter library loan (ILL) is a wonderful tool for researchers, especially those in small centers far from major research libraries. The key to using ILL effectively is to plan research in such a way that it is possible to get through sources efficiently without having too many items out at once. Most ILL can be ordered online now through our home libraries. Imagine how long it might take to get an item and how long it will be useful for and then do not over-order. There is nothing worse than having numerous items show up at the busiest time of the year and then to be unable to get through them in a timely manner. Remember also to read closest to the given topic first, as bibliographies of the most recent research and writing can be mined to keep us from getting too far afield. It is better to wait for an ILL item that is exactly what is needed than to read outside that narrow field for more general information. Start with the most pertinent sources and then work out in concentric circles of generality.

Most universities provide faculty with some kind of professional development funds. One of the best ways to use these funds, or to use outside funding, is by hiring a research assistant. Although one might argue that it is hard to find such a person in a strictly undergraduate institution, for instance, there are often bright and resourceful students who would like to help professors with research projects for modest pay. Consider bibliographic control, scanning or finding particular resources, or help with technology and formatting of work which can be ideal for a research assistant and free up the faculty member for more important tasks. This also provides an excellent mentorship opportunity for students, who often thrive on tasks that are often dull to the average faculty member. Talk to your school's research office about how collaborative work with students could enhance your research program. Alternatively, if your funding allows, hire a postdoctoral researcher in your area of specialization. Although you might not be able to afford full-time help, there are many doctoral students or postdocs who would enjoy providing research assistance, and it will help them in their own job searches to have this under their belts.

One thing to remember is that academics are primarily hired, promoted, and rewarded on the quality and quantity of their peer-reviewed research. As much as one may get carried away with teaching, or want to help out colleagues on important service projects, the core of the job is research productivity. No one can do this for us; we have to carve out the time, energy, and commitment to honor this part of our responsibilities to our disciplines and our universities.

Chapter 4

Teaching

A major focus of this book is to find time and space for "work" and personal time. That is because these are elements that often get squeezed out of a heavy schedule. However, it would be a mistake not to take teaching as seriously as these other areas, because this is realistically how we spend much of our time as academics. Like other areas of our lives, the more advanced planning and organization we can bring to our teaching, the better and more pleasing this role will be. It is worth front-loading the work so that we have more time later in the term and deal with fewer student questions.

The first place to start is the syllabus. Although many of us are asked to throw a syllabus together in short order, or on a topic about which we are less knowledgeable, there is no reason why it cannot be organized. If possible, revise a syllabus or course immediately after teaching it, around spring graduation or in December, when grading is over. This saves time and energy in a number of ways: first, what went right or wrong is fresh in our minds and, second, we will remember things like changes of call numbers or information whose inclusion in the syllabus would have been helpful.

A complete well-ordered syllabus for an average course can run to twenty-five or so pages, although it does not need to. A long syllabus has space for all the information students should know and becomes a helpful lifelong learning document for everyone who takes the class. Syllabi can either be printed on paper or uploaded electronically into a course management system. The first page should include important information, such as on the example in figure 4.1.

Note that the first page not only includes the instructor's email address but also indicates times for email or text office hours (highly recommended because we can do this from anywhere). Textbook information, the all-important grade breakdown, and dates by which the course can be dropped without penalty are all important components of the first page. On subsequent pages, outline the most often-asked questions for any course: the letter grade to number grade correspondences, the policy on late work, how the course will unfold (a brief description of whether this is a seminar course, a lecture course, etc.), and information on reserve lists and where students can get assistance with problems of various kinds. The third or fourth page should list a breakdown of the weeks by theme. This is particularly helpful when introducing the course to students, as the outline can easily be cut and pasted onto

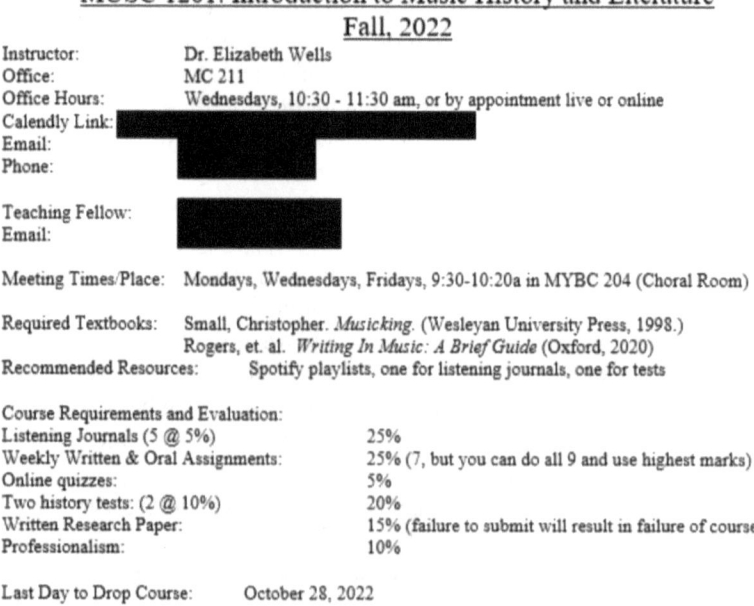

Figure 4.1   Syllabus First Page.

a PowerPoint slide and be presented at the beginning of term. On this page, include due dates and times of assignments and tests; it is very important that the time of day at which something is due is clearly indicated. Also include any foreseeable instructor absences when class may be canceled. This gives students a quick summary of all information on due dates and class meeting times.

The following pages should include a detailed look at readings and other assignments for the syllabus. Figure 4.2 shows a typical "block" from a course.

It is not necessary to include extra readings (e.g., summer reading and listening) on these blocks as they get rather long, but it is important to include everything that is expected for that day, including a reiteration of due dates. At the end of the syllabus, devote a few pages to the assignments and papers that are going to be used to assess students. It is well worth it to think through these assignments in great detail so that students can ask questions about them on the first day of classes, and they can reasonably be said to be "assigned" as of that time. Students can work at their own pace to complete these assignments throughout the term.

After any pages that detail assignments and tests, consider including a summary of important terms, a document on how much study or work might be involved in the course, and helpful information on earning and losing participation grades. For the very organized, and for those who have taught the same course on more than one occasion, include handouts in the syllabus so that it is a complete package that students bring to class with them each day. Simply assemble the handouts for

---

Week 3: Medieval Music: Genres and Styles

September 19, 21, 23 (MWF)
Listening Repertoire: Hildegard: Ordo Virtutem, V. 1, CD 2
(both on CD 444)   Machaut: Ma fin est mon commencement, V. 1, CD 2

Required Reading: Medieval section (Moodle)
    Musicking, Chapter 2: A Thoroughly Contemporary Affair &
    Chapter 3: Sharing with Strangers
    Writing In Music: chapters 1 and 2
Assignments: MYB Conservatory Ethnography Project #3 Due Friday, Sep 23rd OR
    A Response to Art Assignment #4 Due Friday September 23rd
    Online quiz on week's material (including Friday) due Sunday, 8 pm
Monday Symposium: Library Catalogues (in Choral Room)

Remember, you only need to do 7 written assignments, not all 9

Figure 4.2 Syllabus Block.

use, label them according to the day in the term they will be used, and then bind them into the syllabus. They can also be uploaded to a course management system, but putting everything together in a hard copy package with a nice cover and spiral binding sets a tone of professionalism—and even grandeur—to a course.

Also very important to include in a syllabus are instructor expectations and checklists for assignments. In complicated courses, every weekly assignment may be unique. In this case, it is worth including detailed instructions in the syllabus. Although some might consider this "spoon-feeding" students, most students sincerely want to do their best on assignments, and they will ask plenty of clarifying questions in class or over email if we have not provided enough guidance in the syllabus. Although it might seem that this syllabus work is overwhelmingly detailed, it pays off on the other end. In courses with detailed syllabi, students rarely have questions in class, during office hours, or over email about clarification of assignments. Even in very large classes, organized professors can expect not to receive *any* emails from students regarding clarifying the work in the course. If we do not have time to provide this information in detail up front, do we really have time to reiterate it endlessly in emails to students later? This is one of the best time investments teachers can make.

Figure 4.3 is an example of a complicated "listening journal" assignment providing a helpful grading rubric.

In addition to the guidance provided in the syllabus, consider making short instructional videos or podcasts about the weekly assignments. Despite detailed instructions, sometimes there will still be students who want to go over assignments in class. Their visually oriented classmates can be frustrated and may tell these students that everything is in the syllabus. However, these confused students are usually verbally oriented and just need someone to tell them out loud what is expected. As an experiment, one professor went out for a spring morning with a friend and a video camera and filmed short, 2-minute videos on each assignment, in appropriate locales around town. There were no scripts or retakes. She spoke for a few minutes—as she would in class—to describe the assignments and their purpose and then uploaded the videos to the course management system. Although she initially doubted the students would actually watch these videos, it turned out that students in other courses were watching, too. The other benefit is that videos can be watched any number of times, and at any time, so that

Listening Log Rubric

We **will** use the rubric. When your listening logs are marked, check them against the listening journal rubric. If you have questions, feel free to contact Dr. Wells or Gibson.

Notice that the rubric is not geared as much towards what is *not* done for those marks as what *is*.

	A	B	C	D
Basic piece information	Includes basic information about dates, composer, scoring, performance listened to.	There is no good reason not to have an A in this section.		
Research	-Demonstrates concise research relevant to the piece. -At least **two** credible sources regarding composer history, social setting of piece, earliest performances, musical trends of the period. -Research is perfectly intertwined into the explanations of the piece.	Demonstrates research from at least **one** credible source about the piece. -Research is fairly clear and concise. -Most research connects to the surrounding observations and information, however some appears stand-alone. -Discussion of composer history, social setting of piece, earliest performances.	-Demonstrates research, although not necessarily from an entirely credible source with known writers (ie. Wikipedia, random websites) -Research lacks some clarity and each morsel of research takes it's own sentence or section without connecting to the surrounding information. -Discusses composer history, social setting of piece and early performances somewhat, however with ambiguity, error or irrelevance.	-Demonstrates vague research, perhaps 'off the cuff' or from skimming a bad source. -Half or more of the research does not connect well to the piece or the rest of the paper. -Research is cluttered and unnecessarily drawn-out. -Discussion missing of several of the topics of composer, social setting, earliest performance and musical trends of the period.
Observation	-The journal demonstrates at least three listenings and repeated listenings to important sections of the work. -The author comments on overall structure, musical timbres, harmonies, rhythms, potential programmatic aspects, words, and interpretation, while tying in these aspects to the research concerning the piece. -The writer observes and discusses how the piece relates to others works of its period and genre.	Demonstrates at least two listenings, commenting on overall structure, musical timbres, harmonies, rhythms, potential programmatic aspects, words if present, interpretation of specific recording.	-Demonstrates a good listening to the piece, where some notes have obviously been taken. -Comments on some musical and extra-musical observations regarding the piece, although mostly obvious and apparent ones.	-Demonstrates perhaps only one listening to the piece where the student did not pay close attention or take notes on the piece. -The observations are vague and relate only to surface musical features. -The observations offer little in terms of inference or critical thought and act as stand-alone observations with little relevance.
Thematic Relevance	In a small paragraph, the writer goes in depth into the week's theme and how it relates to the piece, touching also on how the composer's approach varies in comparison to other composers' approaches in the same week. The paragraph should also discuss subtleties in the music that relate to subtleties in the week, if possible.	With approximately two sentences, the writer ties in the relevance of the particular piece to the theme for the week.	In one sentence, the writer makes a general connection between the piece and the theme.	In one sentence or part of a sentence, the writer vaguely connects the piece to the theme, relying heavily on the obvious and displaying no research or in-depth thought about the work.
Language	Demonstrate musical and extra-musical language at a university level. The contents are readable and organized between sections. Paragraphs are in proper structure. There are no typos, or grammatical or syntactical errors.	Includes a good introduction with all necessary information. It is most important to demonstrate an understanding of musical language learned in class. The writing shows a balance of academic vocabulary in all areas of the music (e.g. harmony, structure, tempo, rhythm, etc.)	Vague or unspecific language is used. Does not demonstrate a complete understanding of musical language taught. (e.g. a percussionist may have strong vocabulary pertaining to rhythm and tone, but not harmony or melody).	There is no clear structure to the log ('sewn-up point form'). The writing shows little or improper use of musical vocabulary, relying instead on the explanation of concepts through extra-musical terms or the outright avoidance of relevant observations.

Figure 4.3 Listening Log Rubric.

those who might need a little more help and support can find it whenever they want.

LECTURES AND POWERPOINTS

Many students feel "PowerPointed out" because this technology is used in virtually every university classroom. Although we may sometimes long for the good old days when we used to "teach naked" with just a chalkboard and some overhead transparencies, there are ways to effectively use PowerPoint or Keynote to keep students engaged in our lectures. The key to using PowerPoint well is to use it strategically. Slides should not include the lecture script or too many sentences but instead highlight important points. Correct spellings of names, dates, and terms are essential. As a bonus, no one has to figure out our blackboard handwriting! What we don't want is for students to be madly copying down slides while we are lecturing, as this means they are not actually listening to the lecturer but instead becoming copyists. This is not what an engaged and organized classroom should look like.

Students respond well to instructors who are organized and let them know what to expect. Therefore, the first slide of the day (or the first question, if not using slides) should be "Do you have any questions or concerns from last class or in general?" This allows us to deal efficiently with anything that was not understood in the last class, getting that out of the way before diving into any new material. The second slide or announcement should be what will be covered that day, in what order, and how far the class will get in covering this information. Having a road map allows students to organize their notes and thoughts as they receive the lecture. Make sure that different sections of the lecture are clearly marked with transition slides that indicate moves to a new topic. This gives students a little breather in the middle of the lecture and allows them to properly understand the structure of the class. The second-to-last slide should ask if there are any questions (if not already solicited) and point to a few things students might want to think about as they leave the class. The last slide should briefly preview what will happen in the next class and include any reminders of due dates or other key info. Although some professors like to post their slides online, many others find that this practice makes students less likely to come to class. Another downside: they won't necessarily understand the context of the slides without the accompanying lecture and so get only a marginal idea of what happened in the class. One option is to post all slides about a week before tests and exams. This allows students to catch up on anything they missed but does not leave enough time for them to cram. Remove the slides after the exam and keep them down until the next exam. Remember, lecture material is our intellectual property, and we do not necessarily want it out there for anyone to use or see. (Of course, the decision to post slides is entirely dependent on each academic's comfort level.)

The internet and course management systems like Blackboard or Moodle help us all to be better organized. We can post syllabi, assignments, readings, videos, and links to allow students to explore the course on their own time. Paper handouts should not be necessary as these can easily be uploaded or—if we are very organized—bound into the syllabus. When course planning, we should consider what we want our students to get out of the material, as well as what other instructors who come after us would expect students to know after completing the course. Show colleagues some consideration so they do not have to reteach what students should have learned in the course. This goes for class time as well. Be early for class, with the PowerPoint loaded and dongle at the ready, and be prepared to start on time. Do not go overtime, preventing students from getting to their next class or appointment on time. Some instructors think they are so brilliant, so full of wisdom, that they simply can't stop talking on time. This is utter nonsense. Going late just means that we are disorganized, can't cover material efficiently, or are disrespectful of our students and colleagues. There will be always another class hour to continue whatever we were presenting. Use it.

There is more to daily classroom management than lecturing and using visuals effectively. We may also choose to take attendance or give out points for contributions to class discussion. We should have a form that allows us to track this data as we move through a busy class. Figure 4.4 provides a form to keep track of positives and negatives, as well as to remind the instructor of what needs to be announced in class.

It is not necessary to fill in the form during class (except for taking attendance), but we can quickly jot down a check mark or short comment immediately after class.

The moments after class are crucial for organization. Immediately after finishing up the lecture, someone is likely to approach us to ask a

MUSC 1201: Class Report and Grade Sheet

Fall 2021

Date: Monday, November 6, 2021

Announcements: Preliminary Bibliography due next Friday

Due: Reading Assignment #5

Distribute: "Some Advice on Writing Papers" document

Notes:

Name	Present	Late	Preparedness	Participation	Inappropriate
Atwood, Margaret					
Benjamin, Walter					
Castaneda, Carlos					
Dickens, Charles					
Elgar, Edward					
Fitzgerald, Ella					
Gershwin, George					
Hindemith, Paul					
Ives, Charles					
Johnson, John					
King, Sam					

Figure 4.4 Class Report.

question, to let us know they will be absent for something important in the coming weeks, or to request accommodation of some kind. As we are packing up and exiting a room so the next class can get set up, questions feel, at best, poorly timed. If a student has questions that cannot be answered on the fly, we can ask them either to accompany us back to the office (if we and they have time) or to send us a quick email right away about the request. Both of these options work well and prevent us from dropping the ball on anything we need to do for a student. If there are no students trailing us after class, we can spend five to ten minutes mentally debriefing that class. Quickly go through the PowerPoint or the notes and jot down anything that didn't work or that needs further exploration, correct any typos or inconsistencies on slides, and so on. It is also worth filing the class plan in a folder or a binder along with any other important notes.

When teaching the same class more than once, we can draw a line under the last thing we spoke about, so that in the following iteration we will know exactly how long it took to cover the material and whether the amount of material was appropriate for a single lecture. If not, more can be added or surplus material can be moved to the next lecture. Add a few notes like "would be nice to have a visual or example for this" so that during spring course revision we are reminded of things that we need to change. This time after class is also useful for organizing any papers (e.g., tests that need to be returned to any students not in attendance) and making sure that our bags are fully stocked for the next class meeting. Then, after these few minutes, we can move on to something new.

The first and last time a class meets are the most important points in a course. Research shows that students form an impression of an instructor within the first five minutes of the first class and that this impression colors the rest of the term, including how they are going to approach that person and their work for the course. It is therefore vitally important that our first classes, and the way we start our first class meetings, be as organized and engaging as possible. Start by taking attendance to meet the students and begin learning their names. Print off a copy of the course registrations from the registrar's office and make notes during attendance ("tall with purple hair" or "reminds me of Cynthia"—anything that will remind us of the student's name). This is an engaging way to meet students and put them at ease before getting into the meat of the first class. Although it is worth going over the syllabus on the first class meeting—students are often eager to know what the course will look like—some teachers like to jump right away into what excites them about the field or the most interesting course material. Neither approach is wrong, as long as the class is not tedious for the students.

The other essential class meeting is the last of the term. By this stage of the semester, everyone is tired. It is easy to "phone it in" and use this class for review, catchup, or student questions. Course evaluations may also take place during this last class meeting, so it is not the time to deliver a mediocre lecture. It is best to prepare the last class lecture immediately after preparing the first class lecture, both at the beginning of term. Keep it fresh, engaging, and full of interesting content, even if that content is more of a "review" in nature. In this way, the energy of the class stays high, professionalism remains strong, and the course ends with a bang. If the lectures are prepared early in the term, it is easy to make this last one stellar. Go over the learning objectives established at the beginning of the course and ask students to keep us accountable by making sure that those objectives were met. This might be a frightening prospect for many instructors, but it keeps us honest, and that's an important thing to remember.

GRADING

Grading is possibly the least pleasant part of our job, and no wonder: it is time-consuming, difficult, monotonous, and there is a lot riding on it. Although there is probably no way to make grading more pleasant, it can be done in a more organized way. First, write tests and exams when making up the syllabus. Although testing materials will need tweaking as we teach the relevant course content, we will already have the template and the major questions ready to go. Organize the exam in the following order: factual information, true/false, multiple-choice or fill-in-the-blank, longer-answer questions, and an essay question or two if your exam is essay-based. This allows students to warm up on easier questions and populate their answers with correctly spelled names, dates, and terms that will fuel their longer-answer questions. Calculate how long it should take to complete each portion, and put this right on the exam paper so students can plan their writing time accordingly. Make sure to be in the exam room well ahead of time with an exam bag prepared and something to do during the exam. This can be anything that allows us to keep an eye on the class but not waste the whole time just staring them down—marking for other courses is a good option. As students hand in their finished exams, put them in alphabetical order by last name. This means that when we sit down to grade, they will already be in the order we will enter the grades.

Grade as soon as possible after the event, preferably right after the exam. This prevents procrastination from setting in. Find a comfortable (but not too comfortable!) place to do this and then follow a simple technique: grade each section of the exam on all papers before moving on to the next section. This will save time and energy because we will be in the "mode" of true/false, short answer, and so on. Do the same question on every test and then start again at the beginning with the next section. We can power through a lot of sections quickly by grading them this way. When we get to the longer essay portions, or when grading papers rather than exams, follow a 54321 technique. Grade one paper and then take a (very!) short break to do anything other than grading. Then mark two tests, take a break, mark three, and so on. When we have graded five in a row in one sitting, reduce the workload: in the next section grade four, then three, and so on, all the way back down to one. In this way, we can always say to ourselves, "If I can just grade five of these, then the next time there will be fewer" or "I can grade just one." Once we have graded twenty or more papers in a short amount of time, we will be well on our way to maintaining this momentum, with these occasional brain breaks and some judicious small rewards. Remember to keep the rewards short or we will find ourselves derailed before we have a chance to make real progress. When grading exams, don't bother to add comments. Exams by their nature are meant to rack up points quickly, and it is much more efficient, as well as educational, to go over the exam in the next class period with everyone present than to repeatedly write the same things on exam booklets. During the subsequent class, we can reteach whatever material did not land with students the first time.

When grading papers, consider a rubric like the one shown in figure 4.5. This rubric provides a place to indicate where students gained or lost points and a spot for overall feedback about the essay. We should still put comments on the paper itself, but a feedback summary gives a clear overview of the major issues and successes of the paper.

For grading, consider using the following color-coded system. It is more time-consuming than regular grading but really makes the process more enjoyable, more exact, and more informative. When grading, many instructors find themselves bogged down in the prose and details, at the expense of analyzing the paper's overall quality. Then a student gets back a paper that they feel has been "bled on" with red ink and faces the challenge of trying to make sense of all that annotation. With color-coded grading, we take three passes through the paper. The following handout (provided to the students) explains the system.

COLOR-CODED GRADING SCHEME EXPLAINED

When your paper is returned to you, you will find two things: color-coded grading and a paper rubric sheet with commentary on the back. The former will show you where you did things right and where things need improvement. The latter will detail how you earned and lost grades on the essay/paper. Please read the comments, as they can help you to improve your work as you travel through your undergraduate years. Let the colors guide you as to what aspects of your paper (ideas/facts, structure, or expression/presentation) need the most work.

Red

It used to be that everyone used either pencil or red ink to mark papers. Some people feel like this is "bleeding" on the paper, but I like to see it as a passionate, intense, and engaged color. Accordingly, this is used to mark ideas—your own original ideas, how you assess and write about the ideas of others, and how you make use of factual material. This color shows the essential content of your paper, the building blocks, and what you make of them.

Green

This color is a little more neutral. I use it to mark paper structure. What ideas have you started with, and where have you ended? Do your arguments or evidence build in a logical sequence? Are your paragraphs the right length, and is there a logic to the ordering and shaping of the paragraphs? Should some things come in a different order? Where have you placed your examples, if you have any? Does this help the reader to follow your argument?

Blue

This is an everyday color, and I use it for everyday things. Are your margins, fonts, and formatting correct? Have you included your name, course number, and an appropriate and engaging title on the front page? Is your bibliography in the proper format, and are your footnotes and citations correct? Even more importantly, is your grammar, spelling, and prose correct? Do your sentences make sense? I use this for things we used to call "typos," but it refers to all the nuts and bolts of the essay.

In our bags at all times should be three colored pens; it is not necessary to use the different colors listed above, but try to use colors that make some kind of sense to the reader. In this way, we are always ready for grading. Consider keeping them in a small sandwich bag so that they do not leak or get mixed up with other pens in the same bag. Color-coding means students can immediately see where the essay has issues or needs improvements. This also helps us write the overall feedback paragraph. Using red for feedback about ideas does away with "bleeding all over the paper" syndrome. As a result, students are more likely to be receptive to the comments we have made. They come to see red as positive and not punitive. Although this system initially appears more time-consuming than grading a paper all at once, we will get more out of our grading experiences if we follow this method.

In figure 4.5 you will find a rubric for marginalia prepared by Gary Tucker.

Marginal Notes – Explanation of Abbreviations

In graded essays, these abbreviated marginal notes indicate the type of errors detected (compiled by Gary Tucker). Below are the most common abbreviations I use; for a more complete list, visit:
http://www.mta.ca/faculty/arts-letters/music/academics/guides/styleguide/index.html

1, 2 *(etc.)*	See a numbered note at the end of your paper or on a separate sheet.
?	This passage is questionable or unclear. What do you mean here?
¶	Begin a new paragraph
no ¶	Do not begin a new paragraph. (Too many short paragraphs make your essay read like a newspaper article.)
awk.	Your sentence structure or syntax is awkward here.
colloq.	Colloquialism. The underlined word or phrase may be far out in casual spoken English. It is not acceptable in formal written English.
conj.	And we do not normally begin a sentence with a conjunction.
dang.	A dangling verb participle: one whose subject is mismatched or absent. Rushing to finish your essay, your English is left defective.
ex?	Can you provide an example?
inf.	It is seldom correct to with other words split a verb infinitive.
irrel.	An irrelevant statement
no!	This is a factual error.
n.s.	*Non sequitur* (Latin: "it does not follow"). Your conclusion does not logically follow from your premise.
n/s	Not a sentence
oh?	Can you verify this assertion?
passive	The verb here has been written by you in passive voice, weakening its effect. Active voice is often stronger.
prep.	Prepositions are not usually good words to end sentences or clauses with.
punct.	An error in punctuation
ramb.	Your sentence is rambling, that is, it goes on and on without any concise or centralized structure, an effect which is often the result of piling too many clauses into one sentence, and the present sentence is a fine example of such a sprawling, rambling sentence.
source?	You must cite your source.
sp.	Incorrect spelling
sing./pl.	Your mixture of singular and plural persons produce an awkward result.
subj.?	What is the subject of this verb?
ugh!	An inappropriate, even tasteless word or remark
vague	Your statment needs to be more specific.
v/t	You are mixing verb tenses in this passage.
word	Poor word choice. Are you sure you understand what this word means?

Figure 4.5   Marginalia.

Grading has moved online: many instructors mark editable documents that students upload to course management systems. When grading short papers and assignments, use "track changes" and comments

Student Name:_____

MUSIC HISTORY PAPER GRADING RUBRIC
Wells; Fall, 2021

Grading Scheme: 1/3 of the grade for the paper will be allotted to factual detail, evidence of effective research or analysis. 1/3 will be allotted to the ideas presented. 1/3 will be allotted to "presentation" which is primarily writing style, but also includes correct citation and bibliography styles, typos, professionalism of presentation. A check mark below indicates that this element is adequate; *lack* of check mark means this area is ***missing or inadequate***

Factual and Historical Content:

- ☐ evidence of effective research
- ☐ correct spellings of names, places and pieces
- ☐ effective and correct analysis, poetic or musical
- ☐ adequate historical details
- ☐ adequate number of sources cited
- ☐ fulfills specifications of assignment

Ideas Presented:

- ☐ ability to address existing scholarship
- ☐ originality of ideas presented
- ☐ maturity and nuance of ideas
- ☐ clearness of writing and expression of ideas

Presentation:

- ☐ adequate citation of material
- ☐ correct citation style
- ☐ correct bibliographic format
- ☐ typos
- ☐ grammatical, sentence structure, paragraph structure, etc.
- ☐ professional formatting, printing, binding, etc.

Overall Grade:

Comments on reverse side of this rubric - →

Figure 4.6   Music History Paper Grading Rubric.

throughout. The color-coded grading works best with long, in-depth papers that have more weight to them. Otherwise, the in-text comments in a course management system make for the quickest and most efficient grading, since we can always type faster than we can handwrite. It also means we don't have any chance of losing papers or spilling coffee on them.

Track grades on a spreadsheet that will automatically sum the grades at the end of term. The best time to set up this spreadsheet is the first day after the add/drop period ends. This will give us the most accurate class list we are likely to have for the term. Use the window between the end of classes and the exam to make sure everything is added to the spreadsheet. Calculating participation or attendance grades is much easier to do when we are not tired from grading and madly trying to finish the spreadsheet. Have everything ready to go so there are only one or two grades to add and then sum them for a final grade. It is quite useful to have a rubric of number-to-letter grade conversions, depending on what system the university uses.

Feedback is important to students, and the more informative feedback we can give, the fewer questions or grade challenges we will get from students. In course management systems like Blackboard or Moodle, it is easy for multiple-choice or short-answer questions to include feedback depending on how students answer. Have one feedback note for each possible answer: for instance, "You may have thought this was the right answer because it relates to something else we studied that day. However, the right answer is (b) and this is why." Use the feedback system as a teaching moment to constantly reinforce key course content. We can also leave a feedback answer for the full question, which can be used as another teaching moment. These kinds of answers increase the sense of interaction that students have with the instructor, making everyone feel better about the learning process.

OFFICE HOURS

Universities (understandably) want instructors to be available to students: we should be around to answer questions, to talk about course material, and to help our students solve any problems they may be having with the course. Although office hours are not always mandated by the institution, it is natural to offer a few slots during the week, on different days and times. One of the frustrations of university life is holding office hours to which no one appears. Prevent this by hanging a schedule of available times on the office door so that students can sign up for slots. Consider adding a column on the sign-up sheet for what course the appointment is related to or the general reason for the appointment. This will help guide us in preparing for the meeting. If we find that our office hours are still not well-attended, we can opt for by-appointment office hours or electronic office hours, where we are available on a course management system for a synchronous chat function. Students tend to be very message-oriented, and this can be a great way to answer questions and interact with students without having to sit in an office at particular hours. Many course evaluations include questions about how accessible a professor was outside of class time, so it behooves us to make ourselves available. However, in case no students come during an office hour, have a plan for using the time productively. This is not the moment to surf the net mindlessly or to putter around. Make sure to bring substantial work that can still be interrupted when students drop in. If we plan them correctly, office hours can be among the most productive times of the week rather than time sinkholes. The key is that if we have set up physical office hour times, we must honor them. Even if students don't regularly show up, they expect us to be available at these times, and it is only respectful to be there as promised.

Figure 4.7 is a sample of an office hour sign-up sheet with a place where students can suggest other times they could meet.

TEXTBOOKS

Most instructors get desk copies of textbooks, and it is part of our job to choose texts for our courses. However, it is hard to get around to reading them, especially when updated texts are provided for courses. Trying to read all the textbook options in order to make a final choice for the course is very challenging. The best time to read textbooks is in the last few weeks of class. At this time, we will be tired and research work or class planning will be more difficult for us. Get out textbooks and read them. Not only will this inspire us in the last weeks of class, but it may also provide fodder for the classes themselves, allowing us to stay productive

Teaching

Professor Elizabeth Wells

Office Hour Appointments: Room 212
Fall, 2014

Monday, September, 2014

Time	Name	Course or Subject (if applicable)
10:00 am		
10:10 am		
10:20 am		
10:30 am		
10:40 am		
10:50 am		
11:00 am		
11:10 am		
11:20 am		
11:30 am		
11:40 am		
11:50 am		

Wednesday, September, 2014

10:00 am		
10:10 am		
10:20 am		
10:30 am		
10:40 am		
10:50 am		
11:00 am		
11:10 am		
11:20 am		
11:30 am		
11:40 am		
11:50 am		

I need a different time (Dr. Wells will email you after you fill in below)

Day and time range	A second choice of day and time range	Name/email

If you need a 20-minute appointment, please sign up for *two consecutive times*, if available. If none are available, please email me at ewells@mta.ca to set another time.

Figure 4.7 Office Hours Sign-Up Sheet.

right up to the end of term. When selecting a textbook, find something that will complement, not duplicate, the lectures. Consider the textbook as a skeleton on which to hang the flesh of the course. It is necessary for students to read and understand the textbook, but it is not a complete package without the information that you provide in class. The other advantage to looking at textbooks late in the term is that we can order copies from the university bookstore in good time. Consider putting in book orders when finishing syllabi in the last weeks of term (May or December). This is also a good time to submit syllabi and reserve lists to the library so that their staff can be ready to put items on reserve in good time.

Make good use of the many extras that come with modern textbooks, like online study guides or quizzes, extra material for study, and so on. These will save us from having to come up with such supplemental materials ourselves and will make us more efficient and effective as teachers. Although advanced planning is recommended for most academic tasks, it is particularly effective for teaching. Nothing is worse than frantically trying to get content ready the night before a lecture (often called "chasing a class"). Ideally, all syllabi, handouts, PowerPoints, and lectures are fully prepared six months to a year in advance. In calendar systems like Outlook, one can simply open up the class appointment, attach the PowerPoint or any other materials, and save. Then teaching class is as easy as opening up the calendar and accessing the materials for the day. Although different instructors take different amounts of time to prepare a class, having complete PowerPoints or lecture notes ready means less time spent on the day of class and more time spent on reading, research, or our private lives.

As in the chapter on research, consider having teaching assistants and use them well. All students enjoy lecturing, and even if it takes them eight hours to prepare a class lecture, having students to interact with and a faculty member who can give them detailed feedback after the fact is invaluable professional training. If students are undergraduates who may not have the training to lecture appropriately, consider having them lead a discussion class that you can also attend and critique. Although we often think of students as grading assistants, there are many ways they can help with course management systems, providing support for students who are nervous asking professors for help and dealing with technological issues. Ideally, a teaching assistant will have taken the course before and can pass on valuable knowledge to the students. Part of teaching is mentoring, and by doing so with teaching assistants we fulfill one of the most important aspects of our mission. It's a win-win for everyone.

Chapter 5

Nuts and Bolts

No book about the academic life would be complete without mention of the greatest time sinkhole ever created: email. Although different studies report different data, "knowledge workers" spend on average one-third of their time during the week on email, up to one-half of their time depending on the study. This is staggering. A conservative estimate, then, is that during a three-month research period in the summer, 234 of those hours would be spent entirely on email. That equates to twenty-nine full days or approximately one-third of Research Days. Depending on how much work there is to do, and how much email affects the kind of work that is done, this is a substantial amount of research time. Therefore, email control is absolutely crucial to the academic. How, though, does one free oneself from this electronic monster, especially when so many of the important information, tasks, and communication take place over this medium? Although there are ways to manage email better, the first piece of advice is to limit the amount of email that comes in. Yes, to control the response to email, one must ruthlessly and proactively stop the inbox from receiving so much in the first place.

How? First, analyze briefly what incoming emails are about. This is easily done over a couple of days or a week. Consider these questions: What are the sources of these emails, and what do they ask of me in response? The first line of defense would be to unsubscribe from as many email lists as possible. For many, this means list-servs that are devoted to topics of interest or associations and organizations of membership. Many feel that to keep up with their discipline, they need to be constantly reading posts from other people about it. This is untrue. We were all able to keep up with our research areas in years gone by through newsletters or word of mouth. This is still true. What we find now is that there is an overabundance of sharing information because of how easy it is to send an email or post to a list-serv. If a must-read email is essential to staying informed or connected, see if there is one "digest" version of the posts a day instead of individual emails from each poster. This makes it easy to just scan the emails at the end of the day (or even better, on "recreation day" or during the Weekly Review) to see if there is anything interesting or essential that has been missed. Divest yourself of all list-servs and rely on your friends and colleagues to let you know about something that might be of interest. Often a dissertation adviser, mentor, or even someone retired in your field can send information that seems relevant to your research. At first, it may seem that you will miss out on either the ethos of your academic discipline or important research or teaching information as a result of not being on these lists. However, this is simply not true. And so we eliminate a great deal of email by doing this simple thing.

The next way of reducing email is to unsubscribe from other blogs or advertising services that might send emails. It's not hard to notice that any frequented brand or store will send advertising emails almost daily. For anyone who really wants to know this much about the supplier, simply set a time during the week to browse some favorite sites and see if there are any sales on or other useful information. This is much more productive (and relaxing) than constantly getting emails from them. If the posts are enjoyable, then only read them when time allows and ruthlessly delete these messages after reading. We all have a few retailers that we enjoy, but unless we are looking for something particular on their site, it is best to automatically delete their messages every day when they arrive. This is a kind of in-between method that allows us to take advantage of sales or specials but not spend time looking at the emails every day. If emails from institutions or advertisers show up for no reason, unsubscribe (perhaps set a task in the Weekly Review to unsubscribe) so that all inbox clutter is eliminated.

The other way to avoid getting emails is to ensure when sending that there is enough detail in the email to fully inform people of things they might normally email back about. The teaching chapter of this book recommended coming up with a 20+ page syllabus. This is not a "make-work" project or even unrealistic. It means that everything students may want to email about is found in the syllabus. Do you find that students don't read or absorb information as completely as they used to? Then educate them at the first class meeting, emphasizing that everything they need can be found online and that they will not need to ask many questions about assignments or the course. When teaching five courses a year, a detailed syllabus can mean fewer than one or two emails from students in an average week asking for clarification on assignments or details of those courses. This is not extraordinary; it is because they have been taught where to go to get all the information they need.

EMAIL SIGNATURES

Another way to streamline email and to avoid getting emails in the first place is to create an email "signature" that covers as much of the information that people might normally ask about as possible. Although signatures often include name, address, and contact information, this is also a place to list office hours, availability, and information on current projects. You could include a few citations from recent publications. During term it is helpful to list any information people might need to ask about times when you're checking or answering email. For example, include something like this phrase (in color): "To maintain work/life balance, I do not read or reply to email after 7:30 pm or on Saturdays." When you first put this in your email signature, you may feel that people will judge you for "not working enough." More likely, you will find that many people thank you for doing this, as they feel it gives them also permission to limit their email checking and responding times. It is particularly important to educate students on email habits. If they are told clearly at the beginning of term "I only process email between 3:00 and 5:00 p.m.," then they will know either not to send anything outside of that time envelope or not to expect a response at other times. This will both calm them when they have not received an immediate response and allow them to plan their own time and energy better. It is perfectly fine to tell students that "work" happens only from 9:00 a.m. to 5:00 p.m. on weekdays. They don't need to know work happens far past those hours or on weekends. That is not their business. Let them know that you take your "day job" seriously, but it is just that, a job—not your whole existence. If they email you late on Saturday night, there is no reason you need to respond until Monday morning at 9:00 a.m., but make sure you gently educate them in your response that you do not deal with work emails on the weekend.

The other way to avoid getting email is to answer your emails promptly. Many people get follow-up emails like "Did you get my email?" If you are keeping up with your email correspondence, you should not have anyone email you twice about something. If you don't have time for a proper response to an important or timely email, simply spend 30 seconds writing back to the correspondent saying, "I have received your email and I will get back to you by Friday about this." This allows the person to know that they have been heard and when to expect a response from you.

Another way to avoid email traffic is to use the phone more. We used to spend much more time on phone calls than we do now as we are so used to writing emails even for very short or simple information. No matter how fast you type, you will not be able to type faster than you can talk, and as fast as someone can respond, it is not as quick as having a conversation with them in real time. Every time you think to send an email, pick up the phone instead. Getting in to this habit will remind people that they can phone you as well, and more of your communication will become more immediate, effective, and more human.

Once you have eliminated as much email as you can through informing people and staying available by phone, you have to deal with the emails you do get. The first rule, and one of David Allen's teachings, is that if it would take you less than 2 minutes to do it, do it now. This is especially true for email, where simply responding to messages quickly will be better than letting them fester or sit for ages in your inbox. But be realistic. Two minutes is not 5 minutes or 7 minutes. There are many Getting Things Done timers you can load on to your desktop from online sources. This will start to teach you how short "2 minutes" actually is. But it is very important to get rid of less-than-two-minute tasks whenever you encounter them. The second rule of email management is to answer very time-sensitive or important emails right away. This does not mean that you need to necessarily solve or complete the problems they may present to you. It simply means that you will be able to get a start on them and show your correspondents that you are on top of your email by doing so. The third rule of email is not to write emails on particularly sensitive topics. These should always be handled in person or on the phone if at all possible. Unless legal proceedings would depend on what you have written, or if for some other reason you need to have something in writing, deal with these sensitive issues in another way. It just makes more sense, and as mentioned earlier, it is much more humanizing. If you receive an irate or angry email, simply write back and invite the person to a conversation. Often people write such emails because technology allows them to hide their emotions or avoid face-to-face conflict. However, often the result is much worse than an in-person conversation might have been. Therefore, never reply to an angry or hostile email with another email. This will save you a great deal of time and energy.

On a similar note, never write an email when you are angry, upset, or even mildly annoyed. This is not only because you might say something you later regret but simply because in the heat of the moment you will write things that are much longer and more involved than they need to be. People spend inordinate amounts of time drafting and redrafting emails about things that bother them, when after a couple of days the problem has either been resolved or they feel much more relaxed about it. When tempted to write in a passionate mood, let the emotions pass and write something short and to the point later. And again, it's best to have a real conversation, not go back and forth endlessly with lengthy emails.

Another way of making email more effective and efficient is to put as much information in the subject line as you can. This allows your correspondents to triage your email and to know whether they need to open it now or can wait. Instead of "Meeting" as the subject line, write "Reminder of meeting on Thursday, 9:00 a.m., my office." You may not need to even put anything into the body of the email if your subject lines are substantive. Along with making it easier on the people who receive your emails, this will also allow them to easily find among perhaps multiple emails from you the one they want. If your email doesn't need a body and therefore you can use only the subject line, end it with "EOM" (end of message) so the person does not even need to open the email to discern the contents.

CHECKLISTS

In 2011, Atul Gawande, a surgeon and regular writer for the *New York Times*, published a book called *The Checklist Manifesto*. In it, he looked at all kinds of processes, whether they were surgical operations or the building of large complex structures. What he discovered in all this was that all of these complicated systems really ran as a series of checklists, some more elaborate than others. It caused him to come up with a theory that almost any part of our busy lives could be made more effective or efficient with the use of checklists. Although a checklist for sanitizing operating rooms worldwide would seem light years away from what an organized academic might come across, there are still aspects of our lives which could benefit from checklists. A few examples are a "beginning of year" and "end of term" checklist to go through each year, as well as a checklist of conference travel and organization, and "day cards" for daily use at home to make sure your chores stay on track. Even keeping a checklist for every day, including "wallet, keys, lunch,

Conference Title:	
Dates:	
Travel Dates:	
Pre-Acceptance ❏ Start Conference File ❏ Check A/V and all other requirements that are requested with submission ❏ Date Abstract due: _____ ❏ Date Abstract submitted: _____ ❏ Confirmation of abstract received ❏ Price airfare (see reverse) ❏ Price hotel/accommodation ❏ Price local transportation (hotel, airport, rental car) ❏ Price conference registration fee ❏ Finalize budget	**Funding Application** ❏ Bell Faculty Fund deadline? ❏ Other funding deadline and procedures ❏ Does someone need to endorse application? ❏ Write funding application ❏ Application submitted: _____ ❏ Confirmation of application received **Funding (if successful)** ❏ Register for conference online ❏ Book accommodation, local transport, airfare ❏ Complete airfare administration form ❏ Write paper/presentation
Acceptance ❏ Forward email to Financial Services/Provost's office ❏ Send bio to session chair ❏ Confirm travel, accommodation, registration costs ❏ Send A/V and other requirements **Two days before:** ❏ Taking computer? Memory key? Clicker? ❏ Passport ❏ Confirm ride to airport, check flight status ❏ Get cash ❏ Take business cards and C.V.s ❏ Email paper/presentation to self **Four weeks before** ❏ Send updated abstract ❏ Send bio to session chair and head shot, if needed ❏ Confirm A/V needs ❏ Arrange house-sitting, pet-sitting, etc. ❏ Print off all hotel reservations, airline itineraries, driving directions for file	**After** ❏ Follow up emails/phone calls ❏ Send outs to people asking for paper ❏ Send out "thankyous" to conference organizers ❏ Add new business cards/contacts to Outlook and any other address/contact directories ❏ Write funding report ❏ Write project report (if applicable) ❏ Process receipts and do travel expense claim form ❏ Submit all forms and reports _____ ❏ Amount of reimbursement: $_____ ❏ Reimbursement received ❏ Check online financial reports to ensure reimbursements and amounts charged ❏ Check airline/loyalty reward miles credited ❏ Update C.V.

Figure 5.1 Conference Checklist Part 1.

snack, and water," can be quite helpful so you don't walk out of the house forgetting anything early in the morning. You can find a conference checklist online at www.theorganizedacademic.com for printing and below as figures 5.1 and 5.2. Among the checklists on the site are a travel packing list, meal planning and shopping lists, a paper grading rubric, a presentation grading rubric, a "professionalism" rubric, and a checklist for student undergraduate humanities papers. Other checklists you might want to develop for the academic year include "May," "Finalize Syllabi," "Finalize Course Reserves," and "August."

Travel Planning

Air	Rail/Bus
Departure airport code:	Departure terminal code:
Arrival airport code:	Arrival terminal code:
Flight time options:	Departure and Arrival time options:
Price:	Price:
Confirmation #:	Confirmation #:
Notes:	Notes:
Car	**Budget Development**
Driving directions:	Transport to Airport/Station: _____
Car Rental (if applicable):	Parking: _____
Mileage:	Airfare: _____
Price:	Train/Bus/Cabs: _____
Confirmation #:	Car Rental: _____
Notes:	Per Diem: _____
Public Transit/Walking Routes/Cabs	Conference fee: _____
Directions:	Tours, extras: _____
Approximate costs:	House-sitting or pet care expenses: _____
Notes:	Other: _____
	TOTAL: _____

Figure 5.2 Conference Checklist Part 2.

PASSWORDS

In the current age, internet security asks us to create longer and more complicated passwords than in the good old days, where the name of a favorite pet or family member used to suffice. You will therefore need to keep track of passwords in a place that is reliable and secure and which you can access on demand whenever you need to. Programs that randomize and save passwords for you are the ideal solution to password issues. If you don't have the patience for this, simply create one place on file cards or a document (unfindable by others) where you keep all passwords for all sites in one place. A good idea is to put this on an "agendas" list for "Personal Assistant." Put here all passwords and logins, passport numbers, account numbers for budget items, and conference call-in numbers and PINs. Never put in here banking or credit card information and mask the identity of the websites listed in some way in case the list is mislaid. In addition to listing the passwords, also indicate when the password was last changed, as a tickler to change some of those when enough time has passed.

FILING

Although we might have less paper than we used to, most of us still get far more paper accumulation and digital files than we would like. The trick to getting efficient and organized around filing is to do it in the first place. For physical filing, the best is a top-quality four-drawer filing cabinet in which case you can probably comfortably file most of your written records. If you are collecting sensitive information, as in surveys or qualitative research, you should have a locking filing cabinet. Indeed, many research ethics boards will require you to have a locked system for filing personal information about informants or survey participants. It is worth it to spend as much money as you can afford on a proper filing cabinet, even if your school will not provide you with a top-quality one. A beautiful filing cabinet with smooth operation will make filing more attractive to you as well as keep your files in order. Although some experts, like David Allen, recommend filing entirely alphabetically, this can be onerous for people keeping track of filing according to multistep projects like research projects or lab results. Therefore, it may be better to organize by drawer, with one or two projects taking up one drawer (of course, the space that this takes will depend entirely on the size of your project). If you are working on a book or a dissertation, for example, you will need to keep your materials organized in as few files as you can but as many as you can afford. Here's an example of a filing template for a dissertation, which was on the musical *West Side Story* (table 5.1).

On the second line of the original file folder labels—and it is worth it to format and print these labels formally, not handwrite them—was the word "DISSERTATION." This means that if that file ends up being used later for another related research project (which it was), it is easy to know where to return the file. It is not just a matter of organizing

Table 5.1 Conference Checklist

| *Cut Numbers Project* | *WSS Premiere—Clippings and Reviews* |
DISSERTATION	DISSERTATION
Chapter 4—Drafts	Chapter 4—Final Copy
DISSERTATION	DISSERTATION
Chapter 5—Drafts	Chapter 5—Final Copy
DISSERTATION	DISSERTATION
Chapter 6—Drafts	Chapter 6—Final Copy
DISSERTATION	DISSERTATION
Chapter 7—Drafts	Chapter 7—Final Copy
DISSERTATION	DISSERTATION
Chapter 8—Drafts	Chapter 8—Final Copy
DISSERTATION	DISSERTATION
Chapter 1—Research Materials	Chapter 2—Research Materials
DISSERTATION	DISSERTATION
Chapter 3—Research Materials	Chapter 4—Research Materials
DISSERTATION	DISSERTATION
Chapter 5—Research Materials	Chapter 6—Research Materials
DISSERTATION	DISSERTATION
Chapter 7—Research Materials	Chapter 8—Research Materials
DISSERTATION	DISSERTATION
International Reception—Clippings	Chapter Outlines
DISSERTATION	DISSERTATION
Articles from Chapters	Russian Problem—Notes, Articles, Clippings
DISSERTATION	DISSERTATION
Artwork and Photos	Permissions
DISSERTATION	DISSERTATION
Blitzstein	Weill
DISSERTATION	DISSERTATION
Stravinsky Connection	Lectures and Handouts
DISSERTATION	DISSERTATION

research materials, as you can see. It is a way of organizing one's thinking about the project, because the files you choose to create, and the materials that you file in those folders, have to do with one discrete idea or concept that you want to explore (perhaps even later in more detail). These dissertation files, although there will be a point when you are far from your dissertation now, still provide fodder for projects related to the original project.

TRAVEL

One of the joys and also the frustrations about the academic life is the amount of travel we do. Whether it is to conferences, workshops, or archives to do research, academics travel a great deal of the time, and becoming a seasoned and organized traveler is one of the most important things we can do to make this necessary part of life a little easier. Certainly, air travel is not as glamorous as it once was: we are often delayed, baggage can get lost or damaged, and airplanes are just not particularly comfortable places to be. However, an organized traveler can make the best use of the time on trains, planes, and buses, and in fact these conveyances can be some of the most productive places to work. The first thing to remember is to use a travel agent for remarkable or complicated travel. Travel agents seem like a thing of the past now that we have internet booking that we can use ourselves, but there is nothing like having an agent find flights and book insurance. If ever you find yourself waylaid in a strange country with problems, you can simply phone or email your travel agent, who makes everything right, gets you on different flights, or otherwise speeds you more comfortably to your destination. Giving your agent your frequent flyer numbers means you do not have to keep track of them yourself. Although an agent may charge a fee, it is usually small and well worth it when that person also arranges ground transportation and insurance coverage and provides a detailed itinerary. If you have ever booked with a prepaid travel site online and run into problems, then you have experienced how difficult it can be to get attentive service from some of these providers.

Remember that travel agents can book not just planes, but trains and buses, and can find you the best routes to get to your destination once you have disembarked from your major conveyance. Prepaying everything through a credit card means you don't have to stand in lines in train stations to get tickets and worry about carrying enough cash or room on your credit card and means all your tickets are in one location. If you travel frequently to the UK or from America to other countries, it is a good idea to invest in a NEXUS or similar safe traveler card. Not only will customs and immigration be easier, but you can also get into fast-tracked lanes for security and avoid crowds in busier airports. Even one trip a year can earn you the relatively low cost of these cards in time and frustration.

The most important thing to remember on travel, apart from booking through an agent, is to travel as light as possible. Visit your drug store and buy a see-through cosmetic case, and then buy small containers that can hold liquids, gels, shampoo, and other necessities. Most people can exist for a week with a bag that would fit into the palm of one hand and have everything in there from contact lens solution and a shower cap to shampoo, conditioner, and various lotions. Even if you are checking bags, you should not travel with large amounts of any toiletries; it just weighs you down, and the time it takes you to fill small containers with essentials will reward you greatly in speed and efficiency. Color coordinate your clothing choices and take only a few outfits that can be matched in different ways. In this way you will maximize your outfits and pack less. Do not bring clothing that needs to be ironed if you can possibly help it and roll your clothes instead of folding them (they fit better and have fewer wrinkles this way). Dress in layers so that you can easily adjust to temperatures in different parts of your journey, and if possible, wear black to travel. It does not show dirt and lends a sense of formality to what you are wearing in case you get to a conference and your luggage has not made it with you. The only bulky item that some people insist on traveling with is athletic shoes and workout clothes. Even if you are an avid exerciser, it is better to forgo the gym, and pick up where you left off when you get back. You will not have lost that much fitness, but you will significantly lighten your load by leaving these items at home.

With proper planning, anyone can take a carry-on for a trip of less than a week if they follow good packing procedures. Choose a dark-colored bag with a few pockets that can double as a purse or backpack at your destination. As long as the bag can close, there is no reason to pack a separate small bag to use at your destination. If you pick something that looks professional, you can take it wherever your travels lead you and still look well put together. It's always good to carry a laptop and a charging cord, your phone, and lightweight reading materials. This is the time to get caught up on articles in journals that are by their very nature thin and dense. If you pack books, leave them in your luggage and read them in your hotel room. They are usually too bulky to take on a plane, and you will wrestle with getting large books back into carry-on bags when you arrive.

Also, take your own reusable water bottle, emptied for your time through security and filled up from a water fountain in the airport. This will save you time, money, and energy trying to find bottled water in airports. Hydration is important on long trips, so make sure you are prepared. When waiting in the airport lounge, you can spend time reading your journals and getting caught up on your field when you usually have a longer space of time to think and reflect. When it is time to board, do not jump up when your zone is called and try to get on the plane quickly. You want to spend as little time on the plane as you can, so wait until everyone has been called and then go through the gate. By the time you are on the plane, more people will be seated, and it will be easier for you to navigate the aisles. Finally, use the washroom as late as you can just before boarding to avoid having to use unappealing airplane washrooms. Your first stop when you get off the plane can be the washroom, and you will be much happier if you make bathroom visits your first and last stops when boarding.

Many find plane travel, although physically sometimes uncomfortable, to be among the most productive times for work. This is because you're in an enforced, enclosed "office" with nothing to do but sit and think. Although reading on a plane is always beneficial, it's also good to take a laptop (fully charged before you get on) and paper and pen and use this time to write. If you have Wi-Fi on the plane, and you need it to do your work, this is a perfect environment for productivity. If you get tired of working on a particular project, this provides a perfect time to do some file cleanup on the computer. Don't waste your time in the air or on trains—this is precious alone time that you can use for focused productivity.

IN THE ARCHIVES

For many academics, fieldwork and archival work are essential for our research lives. Being prepared for the archive and organized before your trip starts is the best way to make the most of these experiences. First, you may need a letter of introduction from your department chair or a librarian if you are using a particular archive. Therefore, on the day you decide to make travel plans or to submit funding applications to go to a certain archive, contact your letter writer to make your request. You can craft this short letter yourself, indicating your role at the university, your field of study, and that you are a responsible and experienced archival customer. Before you go on the trip, visit the archive's website and understand completely the rules as to what you can copy (if anything), whether photography is allowed (sometimes it is), and what you can take into the archive. You may also need to register for a library or reader's card, so check out what is necessary in this regard before you arrive. In our world of digitization, it is often very easy to locate a finding aid online, and you should spend as much time planning your trip in this regard as you do in the archive itself. Often we have limited time to spend in an archive, therefore prepare your list of items as completely as you can before you leave home. Once at the archive, check into your accommodation and take as little as you can with you to the location. You are often asked to check bags and backpacks or to store them in lockers. This is not the time to take everything you may want with you at all times but the minimum. In many archives, you are not allowed to take any books, pens, or backpacks or bags into the space. Therefore, the best way to equip yourself is to wear a vest that has many small pockets, such as the popular "Vest of Many Pockets" from Tilly. You should carry in the pockets the following:

Glasses and magnifying glass
Pencils and erasers (preferably mechanical pencil that doesn't need
  sharpening)
Tissues
Phone
Chargers
Dongles
Memory keys
Post-it notes (small)
Post-it bookmarks (if allowed)
3 × 5 file cards
Change
Your wallet

Letter of introduction (if not already sent to archivist electronically)
Your library or reader's card (outside your wallet)

You should then be able to walk into the archive with a laptop or iPad in your hand and nothing else. It is easier to go through security and easier to go to the bathroom or to lunch if you have just one valuable that you are carrying. There is always downtime in archives while you wait for material. Use this time to fill out slips for call numbers you would like to request and to write out research questions you would like to consider since the last time you took notes. It is also helpful to create a running list in a spreadsheet or table the call numbers or files you have looked at. You will want to remember this the next time you visit the archive or as a prompt to matching notes up with call number items. You can create this list on the plane on your way to the archive, in your hotel room the night before you arrive at the collection, or while waiting for materials.

Copy as much material as you are allowed in an archive and that you have time to copy. Although notes are wonderful, nothing is as valuable as an original document or materials that you can refer to when you get home. And even though archives duplication can be costly, imagine what an extra night's accommodation would cost compared to being able to finish up a day early and taking those copies back with you. This is especially true for microfilm.

GEAR

Every academic enjoys gear—specialty items that they can use for their teaching and research practices. The main item that everyone needs is a good bag or briefcase. Although the gold standard for such items (and for pens, folios, pencil cases, etc.) is the company Levenger, some may not be able to afford that level of quality. If you can find a way to finance them, Levenger's many products are excellent and are aimed at the sophisticated reader. Regardless of where you source your briefcase or bag, ensure that it has several pockets; a place to put your phone, wallet, and keys where you can get at them easily; and a dedicated space for a laptop. Business travel is made much more pleasant when you have a carry-on sized briefcase or bag that will fit under an airplane seat but is also large enough for papers you need to grade and books for class or your own personal reading. For teaching, have a separate bag for each course. You do not need to purchase bags for this purpose (although one organized academic ordered the popular Lands' End bags with monograms for each class). You can simply use conference bags that you get as takeaways from conferences, if they are cloth or good-quality plastic. In each bag, you should have the following:

A binder (small) with class lists, papers, and so on, for the class and an extra copy of the syllabus
Dry-erase markers (if you are using dry-erase boards), otherwise, chalk in a chalk holder
Pens in red, blue, and green (see ideas on color-coded grading in the teaching chapter)
A mini stapler (easy to find at office supply stores)
Extra paper and file cards (for students who might need them)
Tissues
Dongles or connectors
Memory key
Golf pencils (a handful in an elastic band)

The reason to have one bag for each class is so that you can just grab an organized and complete set of tools and go without having to transfer things to another bag. Of course, if you have a pencil case to keep your chalk, markers, and pens in, you can easily transfer that from one bag to the other, but it's preferable to have separate tools for each bag. It may also be helpful to have an "exam" bag. In it keep golf pencils (for people who forget their pens or pencils for an exam), tissues (students are always needing tissues in exams for some reason), a stapler, and blank exam booklets. Also put into this bag any other items that you might need for the exam. As the students hand in their exam booklets, put them in alphabetical order by last name (there is usually time to do this as they come in) so they are ready to grade in order and therefore easier to enter grades on a spreadsheet (as suggested in the teaching chapter). Then you just take your exam bag with you wherever you do your marking, and you have a discrete work bag with everything you need.

To make checkout at the library reserve desk easier, a good trick is to photocopy the bar code from your library card, cut out that small piece of paper, and tape it onto the outside of each bag. This way the library attendant can simply scan the barcode, and you don't have to take your library card with you for every class. Some libraries may demand that you show the entire card, but if the library staff know you, they may be just as happy having the code to scan easily.

For pens and pencils, nothing beats the mechanical pencil, as it does not need to be sharpened and makes a nice line on the paper. Although some academics like fountain pens, they may not be practical for everyday use as the ink can leak, and naturally this causes problems. It really is worth it to get the nicest pens you can afford. A good and satisfying writing implement goes far in making your day pleasant and your work aesthetically pleasing.

Having dongles of various kinds to plug in a laptop is becoming increasingly important, as laptops are now regularly brought to the classroom and have to be plugged in. It's not necessary to have a dongle or HDMI adapter in every teaching bag (this would become expensive) but instead to keep one in a bag that you carry with you everywhere. You never know when you will need an adapter, so keep one on your person at all times. The same goes for slide advancers for PowerPoints. These are small tools that you will appreciate having when you are lecturing, and it would be beneficial to have one on with you all the time.

PLANNERS

Considering all the standard planners and electronic planners, a good option is to use a combination of Outlook (which is what many universities supply) and a paper planner called the Full Focus Planner by Michael Hyatt. Hyatt is a public speaker and productivity coach who produces podcasts and short courses on productivity and goal setting. His planner was the result of a number of years of experimentation and never finding the planner that satisfied his needs. This is the gold standard paper planner. It includes a section at the beginning for identifying goals, a yearlong calendar, individual pages with room for writing down morning and evening routines, and a place to plan for relaxation on the weekends. Although it is a little pricey (the planners run for three months, requiring you to buy a new one quarterly, or invest in a yearlong subscription), it is well worth spending the extra money. Not only can you identify your most important professional

Nuts and Bolts 83

and personal goals, but you can also keep track of details of your work, appointments, and whether you are achieving sufficient work/life balance. As an add-on, you can order the accompanying Full Focus Journal, wherein you write about how you experience each day, things you learned, and what you will do differently in the future. Both of these items are high-quality hardcover bound with smooth, good paper. Many academics attribute their greater productivity, success, and mental health to using this planner. Of course, any planner that runs the academic year can work for you; you can even get some free at your university, often published by the student society. The only real rule about a planner is that you should have one.

Although going digital for many of your tasks and processes is convenient, there is something very old-school and satisfying (as well as slowing you down to a reasonable speed) about a paper planner. The Full Focus Planner works well for everyday planning of work, and one Tasks lists and Calendars works well for projects and appointments. The two blend beautifully together. Other academics use OneNote, which is also an excellent program developed for Macs, as well as Evernote for keeping track of data. You really need to experiment with a couple of systems to find what works best for you, but you can also use the tools your university supplies for free and get the same level of productivity out of them when leveraged correctly.

You might also want to think about your cell phone. Walking around campus, on your commute, or any time you need a break, you can listen to your favorite music or podcasts on the go. Earbuds make this a discreet activity, although you can also splurge and get nice larger headphones for your downtime. Since we spend most of our days reading, it is refreshing to change modalities to listening for short periods, and this can be a refreshing activity to enjoy during some well-earned solitude wherever you are.

For more checklists, rubrics, and forms, please download these at www.theorganizedacademic.com.

Chapter 6

Life

A book about the academic life would not be complete without at least a passing mention of the rest of one's life. Work/life balance is certainly one of the things that we all strive for and which anyone who picks up a book like this might be seeking. Organizing one's personal life, then, is equally important to truly get more time and be able to escape from the academic grind for a certain number of hours each week.

An organized home starts with the same principles that we find in an organized life: space, time, and rituals or organizational behaviors. The practice here ought to be the same as it is for academic life: we must leverage our own time and energy by delegating as much as we can afford. Hire a cleaning service, if possible. Nothing is worse than having only half a day a week to oneself and spending it housecleaning. Try to get a yard service, snow removal, and other services that will save money or time during those periods of the year. Our time is worth it.

Organize days at home just as you do days at work. If Saturday is truly to be a day of leisure (and I hope this will eventually be attainable), then household chores should be tackled on days other than the weekend to truly unwind for at least one day a week. We also don't want our home life to prey on our conscience or attention while at work, any more than we want the reverse. One suggestion, then, to keep on track and clear out the detritus of the everyday is the creation of "Day Cards." Simply put a hook into the wall near the kitchen or an entranceway that is used daily. Write on a 3 × 5 card a series of tasks for that day of the week, punch a hole in the cards, and hang them up. Mondays might be days to remember to take out the trash and put recyclables in their proper location. On Wednesdays, it's watering the plants and doing up a meal plan for the week. Friday is laundry day, and so on. It is also helpful to set aside 15 minutes per day to do "decluttering," which is essentially going through a room and tidying and getting rid of unused or unwanted items. Through doing this for a year, one can go through all old office files, dead copies of syllabi and handouts, and so on, that have accumulated in file boxes in a garage or office. A little bit every day helps to keep things under control. If there are other family members with responsibilities, this is a nice way to coordinate chores.

Keep a small desktop shredder near where the mail goes when it's brought in, and open and either act upon or shred any mail as it comes in. This will help to keep clutter down and to keep piles from accumulating on kitchen tables, and so on. Meal planning and preps for the week are a highly valuable practice. Whether you are on a special diet, or just want to eat better and more economically, doing a 10-minute meal plan on a Wednesday or Thursday is a perfect way to get organized (and things won't go rotten in the fridge). This meal planning form or one like it can keep you on track: http://www.unlockfood.ca/EatRightOntario/media/ERO_PDF/en/Menu%20Plans/MenuPlanningTemplate_en.pdf. Really, there are endless numbers of these forms on the internet to download.

If possible, have fifty-two copies made and bound into a pad at the local print shop—what better way to organize ready-made meal plans for the year? Include snacks, but only buy for the week to avoid waste. On the back of the form, write out a shopping list (organize the list according to the layout of the grocery store to save time) and then when the groceries have been procured, post the meal plan sheet on the fridge for perusal during the week. If meal planning is on Wednesdays, then Thursdays or Fridays are perfect times to shop for the week on the way home from work (and to avoid Saturday crowds).

Meal prepping is also recommended, especially for school-day lunches. It can be too easy to find oneself hungry and foraging for cafeteria or fast food in the middle of a busy day. Reserve time on Sunday (a proposed day of recreation) to meal prep salads and snacks for the week's lunches. It only takes 30 minutes to do the preps, and then it's very easy to just grab one in the morning and go to work. This saves both time and money—money which can be used to hire a cleaning service, for instance. Below is a recipe which is extremely healthful, yet low in calories, and which keeps easily for several days in the fridge: the rainbow health salad. Essentially, it uses every vegetable that keeps well and has some nutrient density and fashions it into a salad with exceptional color and flavor. The following recipe makes four salads, which can be used from Monday to Thursday, with Friday as perhaps an "eat-out" day.

One bag of kale salad mix (must have kale and other nutrient-dense vegetables like shaved brussels sprouts or broccoli slaw) divided into four—this is the base of the salads. Everything else is diced relatively small:

One carrot
Two ribs of celery
A few handfuls of sugar snap peas
Plenty of fresh parsley
Four radishes
One red bell pepper
One cucumber
Some red onion (to taste)
Cherry tomatoes (unsliced)
A sprinkling of pumpkin or sunflower seeds

The vegetables go in one container. Prepare your choice of one can of salmon or tuna, two hard boiled eggs, or some rotisserie chicken breast, and carry that separately as the protein. For the tuna and salmon, mix with a little mayonnaise, vinegar, or lemon juice. Simply assemble the salad (it will be quite large), and add a small amount of dressing, using either the dressing included in the kale salad kit or your own choice. This will keep energy up at work, and it is simply delicious and nutritious. Buy a nice big salad bowl for your office or faculty lounge so that eating the salad is a pleasure. The salads and protein keep fresh in the fridge for four days. Prepping these salads on Sundays or whatever day is your reset/organization day will mean that you don't have to think about lunch all week. Another great boon to the busy academic is the slow cooker. This is especially helpful for those who have families or have classes later in the afternoon. Simply assemble ingredients in the morning and turn it on. Often the slow cooker makes a large volume, which can be used for meals later in the week, and is economical because it tenderizes lower-cost meats.

To save money and time, make your own coffee or tea and take in a thermal container so you do not have to stand in line at coffee shops (unless, of course, hanging out at the coffee shop is one of your pleasure rituals). Carry a reusable water bottle to save money and cut down on environmental waste. Visit large bulk stores like Costco at the beginning of term to stock up on everything you need, so that shopping trips are shorter and less costly during term. Between that and a meal plan that can be glanced at once a week to see what items need to be obtained, you can cut down a grocery shop to 10 minutes a week.

ENTERTAINING

One of the joys of a personal life is getting together with friends and colleagues over a meal or libation. In the early years, when both money and time are tighter, it is hard to entertain with a full meal at home. We usually tend to go out with friends, but that adds up to both calories and money. Another option (and this is good for busy administrators, as well as harried faculty) is the "cocktail hour" dinner party. Simply get a large brie, a baguette, some pàaté and a few grapes, and two bottles of wine. Invite friends over from 4:00 to 6:00 p.m. on any night and enjoy company and snacks. Baking a brie is a magnificent experience and takes only 15 minutes. All guests will be sated, the wine will be buoyant, and at six they can either stay and order a meal together or go about their own busy lives and commitments into the evening. This will result in just as good companionship and conversation as a traditional dinner party, with half the time and expense. Many academics can fit in a few hours after work for this kind of entertaining even if they have children in tow (make snacks friendly for the little ones), and it keeps everyone feeling sane and socially nurtured even during the busiest of times. And, it will be much cheaper and more pleasant than hitting the local bar during a normal happy hour. Save dinner parties for Friday nights or Saturdays, when you don't have classes the next day. Potlucks are often a great way to save money and engage friends in pleasant conversation and community.

CLOTHING

One of the things we do not like to think about much is that our students notice how we look and what we wear. From a university professor who wore a different fancy necklace every day to clearly color-blind instructors who mixed and matched clashing outfits, the way we dress for teaching does get noticed. One way to simplify the process of getting ready in the morning and not overusing the same outfits is to come up with thirty or so "best outfits" from your wardrobe. Although this may sound insanely micromanaged, what better way could there be to start a busy day but to know what you will put on, that is clean and ironed, that can even be laid out the night before. Make your wardrobe choices professional, and make sure they are in good shape and dry cleaned, if that is necessary. Then make up a list of outfits for all the teaching days in term and follow the list. On laundry day, just check what's coming up that week, and make sure it is ready to go. As long as you do not wear the same thing within a six-week period, no one will notice a reused outfit. Planning this way can also indicate if you need to update any items or if you can get rid of unused clothing. A declutter of clothes to donate to a local charity might be just the thing to keep your home and mind more clear and allow you to focus on more important things.

MONEY

Banking and paying bills have never been easier or simpler. If you have not already done so, automate all your bill payments so that they are directly drawn from your credit card or bank account when they are due. If using a credit card for convenience, or if for collecting points, also automate the paying of the credit card with your bank. This way you get all the points but pay your credit card on time. If you need to pay cash for certain products or services, take out all the cash you need at the beginning or end of the month when you get paid. Use your own bank or ATM to avoid bank charges and thus also skip having to go repeatedly to a bank machine to get cash. Keeping a budget projection for each month or pay period should indicate to you (after consulting your calendar) how much cash you might need for specific events. If you donate to a charity, see if the payments can be automatically debited from your paycheck, so that your tax information is ready for your filing your return. Take a day in the first week of January, when there is probably not much academic work going on and collect and collate receipts from the previous year. This way, when your other tax information forms arrive later in January or February, you can easily do your taxes early or take them to an accountant well ahead of tax season. For tax-receiptable expenses, simply keep a cardboard box and dump all your receipts in there each week when you clean out your wallet or return from a medical appointment. Then everything will be in one place when it is time to organize your information for tax time.

ROUTINES

One of the most powerful suggestions overall in this book is to become a morning person if at all possible. There are many reasons for this. The most important is that no one can get to us early in the morning. Apart from family members who might rise early, or a dog, who needs a walk there is no one who is going to phone, stop by, or email early in the morning. The weight of the day has not yet set in with its many problems that tend to cloud our consciousness in the evening hours. We are fresher and, perhaps with some judicious use of caffeine, able to start the day on our own terms with more energy and focus than later in the day. In popular recent books like *The Five AM Miracle* by Jeff Sanders, writers have been promoting the idea of getting up about two hours earlier than required for work and making the most of those hours by reading, exercising, meditating, or doing a number of other useful activities that often get forgotten in a busy day. Although going to bed as early as needed to get eight or nine hours of sleep may mean that there is not as much time for socializing or relaxing in the evening, this is worth experimenting with. Try getting up earlier than usual (unless already a morning person) for a little while to see how it feels. Along with the early rising, which offers some peace and quiet to the start of the day, incorporate some routines that are beneficial to individual academic practice. The first is meditation.

Meditation comes in many forms and styles, but the central conceit of all practices is to still one's mind and body for a short time to maximize overall focus and energy. A reasonable morning practice of 10 minutes and an evening practice of 20 minutes are possible for most people; try to do more on the weekends if you can. The brain rewiring provided by meditation is well-documented, but many people who have been meditating even for a short time report improved memory, concentration, and relaxed engagement throughout the day. It can be hard to still one's mind, but there are many accessible apps or videos of guided meditation to start with, and as practice garners more control and better results, it will become easier. Remember, this is not a time to think about work, and if thoughts of work intrude, just gently observe them and let them slip away. It may help to visualize a strong but gentle ocean wave surging into your head and taking out with it the many distracting thoughts that come. As the waves come in and out, more "debris" is cleared. Some people use a mantra when meditating. What meditation includes is really up to the individual, but with a little practice it can become an indispensable part of the day.

Along with meditation in morning and evening, including exercise at least three times a week will help you to relax and focus. Less than a quarter of the population takes any regular, consistent exercise, and this is a great shame. Few things can energize the mind like aerobic activity such as jogging, swimming, brisk walking, or a treadmill or other machine of choice. Start small, with 15 to 20 minutes and then build up to 30 minutes or so. Although this is recommended every day, it's easy to get away with a few times a week and still gain great benefit. The endorphins that are released during exercise are so enlivening and focusing that it's quite remarkable how an exercise routine can energize academic work. Belonging to a gym or having a fancy routine is not necessary. Simple bodyweight exercises at home or a brisk walk outside can be enough for this life-enhancing activity. And don't worry about "having time"—if we're being honest, it's not too difficult to find the time to spend in exercise resulting in more alert and more focused time during the day, so it actually saves time by increasing efficiency. It also seems to lay down ideas in the mind very well, so a lot of thinking about work can be done during this time, which is also beneficial.

With these activities one might want to think through "routines" or "rituals" that help to define parts of the day. Not only are these centering practices, but they are also routines that help us prepare for the day and also all-importantly decompress from the day. They help to delineate the "not working" time, which is as important as the "working" time. A typical morning routine could involve meditation, some gentle yoga stretches, reading spiritual (nonacademic) texts, journaling briefly, doing a fitness routine, and having a good breakfast. Similarly, have a work shutdown ritual to enact in the late afternoon. Shut down email, after making sure to have taken care of anything urgent, perhaps do a quick yoga stretch, and write in a journal about the workday and how you are feeling at the current moment. Try using the handy and attractive "Five Minute Journal" sold online by Intelligent Change, which really only takes five minutes a day, if that. For work journaling, the Michael Hyatt Full Focus Journal (a companion to the Full Focus Planner mentioned earlier) is helpful because it asks the journal writer to assess things read or heard during the day, and often this can be material having to do with work. Taking a few minutes to reflect on academic work is a way to sort it out in one's mind, instead of just walking away at a particular moment.

An evening ritual can also be powerful, especially for those who have trouble sleeping. They may benefit from some herbal tea, a hot bath, and perhaps limiting screen time two hours before bed. Studies have found that backlit devices interrupt normal circadian rhythms, so shutting them off a little earlier might be necessary in order to allow for the rhythm to get back on track. Sleeping in a room which is a little cooler also helps the body adjust to sleep.

It is also good to develop morning and evening routines, making sure that they are not just excuses to work more but actually times to rejuvenate and do something "for you"—not anyone else. Small routines each day will help with getting through a busy week, while maintaining energy, focus, and calm—and we can all use more of those!

A NEW SABBATICAL SYSTEM

Sabbaticals are now fairly ubiquitous on college campuses. Although at some universities they are automatic after six years of full-time service and the approval of a viable sabbatical plan, at others they are earned only after a certain amount of research productivity has been accomplished. Paid at as much as 90 percent of salary or as little as no salary (researchers have to find their own external source of funding to make up the salary differential), they are a gift that keeps on giving. Every sabbatical reaps rewards, from increased relaxation and well-being, to the time to write in large uninterrupted swaths, to the all-important time to think about one's discipline and one's work. The sabbatical is, naturally, modeled after the Judeo-Christian Sabbath, during which six days of work (and in Genesis, of God's creation) is rewarded with one day of complete rest. The system works so well, and is so ancient, that it only seems intuitive to extend it to our working lives as a principle worth following. So, why not adopt this sabbatical system working up from the smallest increments of time to the largest?

For every 60 minutes of work, take 1 minute off. This would mean a 10-minute break every hour, which aligns perfectly with the traditional 50-minute class lecture. It also fits with the Pomodoro Technique, although there the hour is split into the two 25-minute sections with 5 minutes at different points. This is often recommended by health professionals and productivity experts as a way to stay fresh and move the body, especially if one's work is glued to lab work or the computer screen, as much of our work is. For every six hours, take one intentional hour off. This again is not difficult to achieve. Workers who take a lunch hour off instead of working through have been proven to be more effective and efficient at their jobs than those who do not. So take a lunch hour or an afternoon break and another break later in the day (say, a dinner hour or a trip to the gym). It will be restorative and refreshing. For every six days, take one day off. This advice is given elsewhere in this book. It is absolutely vital to take one full day off academic work a week to maintain focus, productivity, and the correct amount of perspective.

For every six weeks, take a long weekend. Sometimes this is afforded by national or statutory holidays; sometimes it might have to be self-designed. Studies show that high-achieving people who take "mini-breaks" or mini vacations every six weeks are much happier and more productive than those who do not. And for every six months of work, take one intentional month off. For academics, this is relatively easy in the summer. But the winter holiday can also afford an opportunity for an extended break. Although it is argued in other parts of this book that the intersession between December break and the start of term in late January is an excellent time for research and writing, it would be beneficial (when at the top of our game) to take some extended time off then. Vacations don't have to be fancy or expensive or involve international locales. A "staycation" can be just as restorative (and sometimes more so). Travel around the world with a new culinary adventure every night, watch movies, and explore your local town or city. The idea is simply to take an extended period off work (if possible) and enjoy refreshing mind and body.

Of course, the next level up is the actual sabbatical, planned every six years (or, if circumstances allow, a half-sabbatical every three years, which can be even more restorative than the every-six-year extended time). The sabbatical system makes a lot of sense on a number of levels. Following it regularly means dramatically improving overall quality of life and not suffering from burnout as often as some of our hardworking (but not necessarily smart-working) colleagues.

Postscript

WHERE DO I START?

After reading this book, you might feel overwhelmed or unsure where to start in implementing what you have learned. Don't worry; getting organized is a process, and you can use my suggestions to get almost everything under control within a few months.

If you're a procrastinator (and let's face it, many academics are), then I suggest that you give yourself an immediate win by doing one project right away. For example, say you have a book review due in a few months that you were going to start closer to the deadline. If you're like me, you like to read books for review quickly and intensely, so that all your thoughts about the work can be condensed into a cogent review. Let's say that you've allotted up to two weeks to do the review, based on how busy you are. I suggest that you *do this task now*. Don't try to complete a project that is very large or difficult to finish. Pick something that gives you a quick win. Complete your review quickly, trying nonetheless to maintain some degree of engaged relaxation, and submit it far ahead of the deadline.

The next step is to start working backward as you finish up work that is due closer and closer to your present time line. You'll have to pause occasionally to meet any immediate deadlines. However, following this pattern will give you that satisfying sense of "working ahead"—and you can take the occasional afternoon off to go to the zoo with your kids without a sense of guilt. Proposals for conference papers or funding applications are also good "do-ahead" projects. Don't work to the deadline; instead, work ahead, and you'll be pleased at the feeling of calm control that comes from knocking off smaller tasks far ahead of schedule. Note how many items on the Planning Document in chapter 3 are "waiting for review." It's a good feeling: you know you've done what you can, freeing you up for more interesting projects while you wait to get finished work back.

A filing system setup or a complete office clean might take you more time, but again, try to get ahead of things: carve out some time to start these projects early in the summer. If attempting a complete office clean feels overwhelming, then just put your clutter in a series of bankers' boxes and store them in a corner of the office, stacked up. You will still feel like you cleared the space, but you can actually go through the boxes and sort them at another time (perhaps with the help of an assistant).

HIRED HELP

Usually academics make enough money, or have access to enough funding, that you can hire a student or other assistant. This doesn't have to be a full-time commitment but one that can allow you to get organized more efficiently. Even if students do not have the wherewithal to do your filing, they can certainly set up a filing system for you. They can also help with office cleanup, with sorting books and articles for you to read, and with finding contact information for your future correspondence. If you find a student who can be both kind and firm, there's a very good chance they will convince you to let go of some things. I had one of these lovely young people a few years ago, and he convinced me to divest myself of stacks of paper journals that I had "saved" when the library went digital. He made me realize that my office was not the reference area of a library, and we threw them out. I never missed them.

I also think that undergraduates can be hired to do simple things like create a database of books (or recordings, in my case) so that you know exactly what resources you have. They can file lecture notes, help to organize course materials, or type up course evaluations. There are myriad time-saving and energy-saving chores that students (or your children, if they are old enough to help) enjoy doing that can help you along in your academic practice. If you have a few hundred dollars, or institutional money, consider using it like this to leverage your valuable research time while giving someone else a bonus.

I once had an academic friend visiting my house with her young teenage son. He was clearly bored, so I asked him to go up to my study and put all my journals in date order (I had recently moved and the dust was still settling). He had fun, I got to have adult conversation with his mother, and he earned himself a $20 bill. Everyone was happy. Imagine small but fun tasks for young people or students like this to get yourself organized. Everyone wins.

My last point—and it's important!—is to take from this book only what will actually help you. You can't necessarily implement all my suggestions and techniques, and you may not want to. But my systems have been developed over many years, every checklist or form or process honed year by year to make my life more organized. By this time, my systems are pretty tight, and I have a lot more time to do things (like write this book) than many of my harried colleagues. You can do this—and what's more, you'll find it fun—if you go about it with realism and optimism.

I hope you've found this book helpful, and I wish you all the best on your organizational journey. We do have one of the best jobs around, and with a little help we can feel that way every day. An organized academic is a happier academic. And that's really what it's all about.

Please reach out to me on my website at www.elizabethwells.ca where you'll find many of my resources and other information on teaching. I'd love to hear about your journey.

Bibliography

Allen, David. *Getting Things Done*. Rev. Edition. New York: Penguin Books, 2015.
——— *Making It All Work*. New York: Viking, 2008.
Bailey, Chris. *The Productivity Project*. Toronto: Viking Canada, 2017.
Bain, Ken. *What the Best College Teachers Do*. Cambridge, MA: Harvard University Press, 2004.
Berg, Maggie and Barbara K. Seeber. *The Slow Professor*. Toronto: University of Toronto Press, 2017.
Covey, Stephen R. *First Things First*. New York: Free Press, 1996.
——— *The Seven Habits of Highly Effective People*. Rev. Edition. New York: Simon and Schuster, 2020.
Gawande, Atul. *The Checklist Manifesto*. New York: Picador, 2011.
Morgenstern, Julie. *Organization from the Inside Out*. 2nd Edition. New York: Holt Paperbacks, 2004.
——— *Time Management from the Inside Out*. 2nd Edition. New York: Holt Paperbacks, 2004.
Mullen, Carol and W. Brad Johnson. *Write to the Top!* London: Palgrave MacMillan, 2007.
Newport, Cal. *So Good They Can't Ignore You*. New York: Grand Central Publishing, 2012.
——— *Deep Work*. New York: Grand Central Publishing, 2016.
——— *Digital Minimalism*. New York: Portfolio, 2019.
Sanders, Jeff. *The 5 AM Miracle*. Berkeley, CA: Ulysses Press, 2015.

Silvia, Paul J. *How to Write a Lot*. 2nd Edition. American Psychological Association, 2018.

Zerubavel, Eviatar. *The Clockwork Muse*. Cambridge, MA: Harvard University Press, 1999.

WEBSITES

www.theorganizedacademic.com.
www.franklincovey.com.
www.unclutterer.com.
https://francescocirillo.com/pages/pomodoro-technique.

Index

academic calendars, 19, 20
academic life: guilt, fear, and shame, xi–xiii, 27, 44; roles and responsibilities, 13–15; as unique, xvii–xviii, 18, 21; values, xvii–xviii, 1–5; work/life balance, xiv, xvi, 30–31, 36, 83, 85
academic week, 24–28
academic work: aligned with values and objectives, 1–2, 5–6; defining and refining, xvi–xvii, xx; self-knowledge for, xx, 1–12, 28, 31; in short intense bouts, 24
academic year, 18–23
Administrative Day, 25–26
Allen, David, xviii–xx, 14–15, 27, 28, 70, 74
archives. *See* libraries and archives
areas of focus, 14–16
autonomy, 3

bags/totes: briefcases, 80; carry-ons, 77; class/exam bags, 50, 58, 81; pocketed vests, 79
Berg, Maggie, 11
blocks of time: concept, xviii; course blocks, 51; week blocks, 24; work blocks, 42–43

breaks and rest: in academic year, 18, 21; on designated days, 27, 85; in grading, 58–59; with music/podcasts, 83; new sabbatical system, 92–94; Pomodoro technique, 42–43, 45, 93
bulletin boards, 45
business/corporate world, xvii–xviii, 1, 18

calendars (for planning), 45, 66, 82–83
calm control, xvi, 16–17, 96
Career Itinerary, 34–36
chairs, 46
checklists and rubrics, 71–77; for conferences and travel, 72–73; for core values, 3; for grading, 52–53, 59, 61–63, 73
Cirillo, Francesco, 42–43
clothing, 77, 88–89
cocktail-hour dinner party, 88
coffee shops: in morning routine, 87–88; as work spaces, 6, 44
commute times, 29, 30, 83
computers. *See* laptops
conferences: bags from, 81; checklist for, 72–73; papers, 95–96;

planning for, 34, 40; travel to, 76, 77; in yearly schedule, 21, 23
course blocks, 51
course evaluations, 22, 57, 64, 96
course management systems, 52, 55, 63–64, 66
course reserve lists, 16, 21, 66, 73
courses and classroom management: debriefing and notes, 56–57; first and last meetings, 57; lectures and slides, 50, 54–58, 66; optimal days and times, 12; professionalism, 52, 57; students' questions, 56; teaching assistants, 66; textbooks, 50, 64, 66; tracking forms, 55, 56. *See also* grading; syllabus; teaching
Covey, Stephen, xviii, 2–4, 13, 27
Csikszentmihalyi, Mihaly, xvii

daily schedules, 28–31, 39
day cards, 72, 85–86
days: best/worst times, 7, 17, 28; themed, 24–28
decluttering: for 15 minutes, 86; in Pomodoros, 43; in wardrobe, 89; of work space, xvi, 44, 96–97
due dates: in Planning Document, 36–37; in syllabus, 51; working ahead of, xvi, 17, 33, 95–96

email: organization, 24–25, 27, 67–69; *vs.* phone, 70–71; second screen/laptop for, 44, 45; from students, 50, 52, 68–70
energy and focus: areas of focus, 14–16; balanced use of, 30–31; personal rhythms and cycles, xx, 7–8, 11–12, 90; for themed days, 24–28
entertaining, 88
evening: routines, 82, 92; as work time, 7, 11, 24

examinations. *See* tests and examinations

fear. *See* guilt, shame, and fear
filing systems, 74–76, 96
finances: automated payments, 89; budgets, 41, 45–46, 89; funding applications, 41, 96; hired help, 44, 47, 66, 85, 96; research expenses, 38; tax documents, 87–90; travel costs, 76–77
food and meal planning, 23, 73, 86–88

Gawande, Atul, 71–72
Getting Things Done, xviii, 24–25, 27, 70
Ghandi, Mahatma, 6
goals: as realistic, 23, 33–34; and self-knowledge, 7–12; and values, 1–6
grading strategies: in academic year, 19–20; color-coded scheme, 59–60, 63; for essays, 58–60; grade breakdowns, 50; marginalia, 62; online process, 63. *See also* courses and classroom management; tests and examinations
graduate school, xi–xiii
guilt, shame, and fear, xii–xiii, 27. *See also* overwhelm

habits, xviii
handouts. *See under* syllabus
hired help, 44, 47, 66, 85, 96
housework, 17, 72, 85–86
humanities, 8–9, 33, 73
Hyatt, Michael, 82

independent work, xvii
influence, level of, 3
interdependence, 3

interlibrary loan, 46–47

Johnson, Brad, 41
journals, personal, 8, 83, 91–92
journals, scholarly, 10, 33–34, 37, 78, 96

knowledge work, xix–xx, 67
know thyself. *See* self-knowledge

laptops: accessories for, 82; passwords, 74; traveling with, 77–78, 80; working with, 44–45
laundry, 7, 17, 86, 89
lectures. *See under* courses and classroom management
libraries and archives: course reserve lists, 16, 21, 66, 73; digital resources, 96; interlibrary loan, 46–47; reader's cards, 81–82; visits to, 76, 79–80; as work spaces, 44

marginalia, 62
meditation, 90–91
mentorship, xvii, 9, 36, 47, 66
missions, mission statements: central significance, 1–2; components of, 3–4; and self-knowledge, 7; software for, 3; types of, 2, 4–5; uses for, 5–6, 13; to write, 6
money. *See* finances
Morgenstern, Julie, xviii, 7
Morning, "morning people," 11–12, 90
Mullen, Carol A., 41
multitasking, 45

Newport, Cal, xix
next actions, 16–17, 41

office hours, 10, 25, 50, 63–66, 69
offices. *See* work spaces

overwhelm: and next actions, xix, 16–17, 95–96; and Pomodoros, 42; and service work, 31

passwords, 74
pens and pencils, 81–82
People Day, 25–26
personal life, 85–94
personal projects, 38
physical activity, 21–23, 29, 30, 77
planners and journals, 8, 82–83, 91–92
Planning Document, 36–41
podcasts, 52, 82, 83
Pomodoro technique, 17, 42–43, 45, 93
PowerPoint. *See* slides
procrastination, 95–96
prose. *See* research and writing
publishing projects, 33–34, 37, 40

Recreation Days, 27–28, 68, 86
religious observances, 14, 27, 30
research and writing: in academic week, 24–28; in academic year, 18–23; in Career Itinerary, 34–36; core values for, 3; in daily schedule, 28–31; in monthly schedule, 21–23; optimal times, 11–12; Planning Document for, 36–41; realistic approach for, 33–34; themed days for, 17–18, 26–27, 30, 67; writing resources, 41–42
research assistants, 17, 20, 38, 47, 96
research mission, 2, 4–6
research program/statement, 1, 5, 34, 47
rest. *See* breaks and rest
retirement, xiii
retreats, xiii, 6, 20–23, 25
roles and responsibilities, 13–16
rubrics. *See* checklists and rubrics

Sabbath, 27, 92
sabbatical system. *See under* breaks and rest
sciences, 9, 33
Seeber, Barbara K., 11
self-care, 23
self-knowledge, 1–12, 28, 31
senates, xv, 10, 18, 19
service missions, 2, 6
service work: activities, xv, 10; considerations for, 3, 28, 30–31
shame. *See* guilt, shame, and fear
slide advancers, 82
slides (PowerPoint, Keynote, etc.): posted online, 55; preparation, 66; revision, 56; strategic use, 54; of syllabus pages, 50
social occasions, 22, 88
spreadsheet tracking: for archival research, 80; for grading, 63, 81
students: email from, 50, 52, 68–70; encounters with, 9–10, 56
syllabus: in course bag, 81; course outlines and blocks, 51–52; detailed content, 49–52, *50*, 68–69; digital *vs.* print, 49, 52; grade breakdowns, 58; handouts in, 51–52, 55, 59, 66; and textbook orders, 66. *See also* courses and classroom management

teaching: activities for, 9–10; in Career Itinerary, 35; clothing for, 88–89; core values for, 3; planning and preparation, 10, 18, 49, 66; themed days for, 25–26, 89; time required, 28, 30–31; videos for, 52. *See also* courses and classroom management
teaching assistants, 66
teaching mission, 1, 4–5

tenure and promotion: files/dossiers, 1, 10, 34, 36; hiring for, 18, 19; and service activities, 31
tests and examinations: in academic year, 19–20, 22; advance preparation, 58; exam bag, 50, 58, 81; lecture slides, 55. *See also* grading
textbooks, 50, 64, 66
themed days, 24–28
thinking (staring out window), xx, 9–11
time, 13–31; blocks of, xviii; as finite, 13; and personal proclivities, 7–8, 11–12, 17–18; windows of, 28, 63
timers, 42–43, 45, 70
travel, 73, 76–79
travel agents, 76
Tucker, Gary, 62

values, xvii–xviii, 1–5

water bottles and thermal containers, 78, 88
weekends: with Fridays off, 39, 93; in summer months, 21, 23; as time off, 27, 82, 85, 90; as working time, 24, 69–70
Weekly Reviews, 27, 41, 68
weekly schedules, 24–29, 38–39
working ahead, 95–96
work/life balance. *See under* academic life
work spaces: decluttering, xvi, 44, 96–97; office location and set-up, 43–46; during travel, 76, 78
writing. *See* research and writing

Zerubavel, Eviatar, 41

About the Author

Elizabeth A. Wells earned a bachelor of music degree from the University of Toronto with a concentration in history and literature of music and completed her doctorate in musicology at the Eastman School of Music. Her dissertation entitled *West Side Story: Cultural Perspectives on an American Musical* was supported by the Presser Foundation and the AMS-50 Dissertation Fellowship. This work was published as a monograph and won the Music in American Culture Award of the American Musicological Society. Her work has appeared in *Cambridge Opera Journal*, *The Journal of the American Musicological Society*, and *Studies in Musical Theatre*. She is former dean of arts and Pickard-Bell chair in music at Mount Allison University in Sackville, New Brunswick, Canada. She has won four teaching awards, including the 3M National Teaching Fellowship and the Teaching Award of the American Musicological Society. Her research interests include Leonard Bernstein, musical theater at mid-century, feminism, and the scholarship of teaching and learning.